The Story of
SCOTLAND'S TOWNS

The Story of SCOTLAND'S TOWNS

ROBERT J. NAISMITH

JOHN DONALD PUBLISHERS LTD
EDINBURGH

To H. A. Rendel Govan

in recognition of the unique contribution he has made to Scottish town and country planning particularly in the Highlands.

ISBN 0 85976 257 2

Phototypeset by Newtext Composition Ltd., Glasgow.
Printed in Great Britain by Butler & Tanner, Frome, Somerset.

The author gratefully records that the work in the study, research, surveying towns, photographic survey, and the preparation of early plans of towns was generously supported by Glenfiddich Living Scotland Awards and The Bank of Scotland.

The jacket illustration, from an original drawing by W. L. Leitch, 'New Assembly Hall, Edinburgh', c.1850, is reproduced by permission of John Nelson, Prints and Maps, Victoria Street, Edinburgh.

Illustrations

(Maps drawn by Stephen Gibson)

Key to Illustrations
WCA W. C. Aitken
JD   James Drummond RSA
WG   William Gibb
DOH D. O. Hill RSA
BJH   Bruce J. Home
JL   J. Leconte, engraver
FCM Sir Frank Mears
(All unattributed photographs are by the author.)

Foreword

It was typically generous of Robert Naismith to ask me for a Preface. He could so easily have said, 'You gave up too quickly and landed it all on me'. And it would have been true.

I was inspired years ago by Sir Frank Mears to follow on from lectures he had given, to look for more evidence of what he had said of nineteenth-century Scotland. I got so far, then realised I had reached retirement age and was losing my sight. All the necessary searching on the ground was impossible. So I handed the manuscript across, and set off with my wife to see as much as I still could of other peoples and how they tackled the problems of domestic living.

Meanwhile Robert Naismith pushed on and it was in this period that we met men who said that maybe Sir Frank had been very wrong and that there was no documentary evidence of the views he had of planned towns in a planned Scotland: it had all just grown naturally. Though these included renowned academics, their lack of vision and imagination was frightening. Did they not realise that writing was rare till later? Or that it takes superior power to make 'these turbulent Scots' toe the line and build in a comely community manner in current fashion, yet providing for future growth?

It is true that fashion has a powerful influence on the tastes of most men and women, and it can be a valuable force towards date and communal style. But it can become dangerous when it is blindly followed by town councils or others who are given power to say how we should build our towns and houses: fashion or slick talk are no substitutes for listening or sensible thinking.

I heard Sir Raymond Unwin in New York. He showed how two-storey terraced houses, each with its small garden, could hold the same amount of people, area for area, as the tall blocks they were erecting with their necessary surrounding open space. There is no excuse for lack of clear thought and finding out what the people who will live in the area really want.

Just now there is a reaction against much of the building of the last twenty or thirty years. It has become fashionable to rail against modern techniques. Much of it is justified and much not. What we must inveigh against are architectural grandiloquence and glib fashion. Both are disastrous.

This book shows so well attitudes of past times which have led to modest, comely and functional design. This modesty of spirit and clarity of vision are what we most need in the future.

H. A. Rendel Govan

Author's Acknowledgements

It has taken three years to produce this present volume, and but for the assistance and encouragement of my helpers it would at the best be still far from complete, or at the worst, abandoned. Flora Kelly managed the business aspect, read my almost illegible manuscripts, typed them and, as I have become accustomed to for many years, gave me far more of her time than I was entitled to expect. Celine Castellino relieved me of a significant proportion of the task to which I had committed myself by researching into books, finding copies of old maps and discovering independently sources of information that I had thought might not exist. Stephen Gibson made clear maps from the early towns out of the results of my complicated analysis. The staff of the National Library of Scotland patiently provided books and maps for study whenever requested, and several other librarians and archivists produced valuable references.

Consent was given by the Society of Antiquaries of Scotland for reproducing Drummond's drawings, and the Edinburgh New Town Conservation Committee lent photographs for reproduction.

The Scotsman and Hunting Aerofilms issued permits for copying their excellent photographs. Necessary assistance was provided in the photographic work by R. Charles and W. F. Naismith.

Lastly, as may be assumed from the Foreword, my friend and colleague Rendel Govan started this book, and much of the first chapter is based on his work. His support, so freely given, has meant a great deal to me.

To all the above I am most grateful.

Robert J. Naismith

Contents

Introduction

All of Scotland's oldest towns were 'new towns' of the twelfth and thirteenth centuries. They were located on sites chosen over a wide area of the country. They were laid out on these sites to conform to well conceived plans. The enterprise was sound because there were few failures, and nearly all the towns (despite the inevitable changes over the centuries) retained their early ground framework. It has shown that towns planned on simple and generous lines are better able to respond to the pressures of gradual evolution. Where such evolution has been guided wisely in the past by the authorities, the historic Dean of Guild Courts, it has been possible to reconcile the newer ideas with the older survivals.

The only constant theme in the evolution of towns is the process of continuous change. Urban institutions and systems of commerce and industry belonging to past generations decline and others emerge to be adopted by the new generations. This process ultimately calls for the adaptation or recasting of the urban fabric. It is not a phenomenon only of our recent times. Over the centuries spaces and buildings have lost their usefulness and have been adjusted and maintained or renewed and replaced. Types of building and their techniques of construction were abandoned and superseded by new models made to conform with newer concepts. Even in periods when the pace of the whole process may seem to have lost momentum, the action of climate still erodes and slowly destroys, while the abrupt calamities of fire, flood and war have been seen to cause widespread destruction, followed by renewal or extinction.

Despite the combined ravages of history and nature, towns which have survived nearly always manage to retain elements of their original framework. Once established, they acquire a stability of form that develops an inherent resistance to complete transformation. The ownership boundaries of land are not easily shifted. Roads and access ways long outlast buildings, and the contours of the surfaces and natural obstacles such as small rivers, hills or cliffs, although nearly always subject to certain urban alteration, are seldom ever completely obliterated.

As towns have grown older, their form and features can still be traced back to the pattern that was assembled in the period of their first few years of existence. This fact is of central significance. No deep understanding of a town in its modern form can be obtained where the capacity of viewing it as a phenomenon in a process of evolution is absent, or where the historic stages in its growth are not known. The mind has also to be conditioned by the same approach in the consideration of the future of a town if change is to be effected naturally. It is better for the future of towns that their modern aspect is recognised only as a 'still' on a film reel. It shows a single image but its significance is greatly multiplied when its proper function is accepted as merely a fleeting impression in the greater urban drama of the complete projection. Sir Patrick Geddes's comment, recorded over sixty years ago, is still valid: the buildings of medieval towns may be shattered or destroyed but 'their influence continues . . . as historic filiation, as social momentum largely determining our lives to this day'. The old Scottish towns can be seen to have inherited their character from the 'genes' with which they were endowed at their births. At every period of renewal and refreshening these inherent traditions may be better permitted to remanifest themselves for the benefit of that general and local character which Geddes pointed out 'was no mere accidental old-world quaintness'. It has been achieved in 'active sympathy with the essential and characteristic life of the place concerned'. How important it is, therefore, to study and understand the matter of character.

It may appear that this concept of towns gives little credit to that other form of urban change – town extensions. Towns, especially the larger towns, have sometimes the power like some plants to produce offshoots.

Experience has shown that such extensions may become greater than their progenitors. In late medieval times newer, separate, more spacious market places would on occasion eclipse the original. In extreme instances such as the eighteenth-century and nineteenth-century extensions of Edinburgh, the original old city suffered near abandonment and severe decay to the point that many of its immediate characteristics of past times became extinct. But it still recovered.

The history of the newer towns in Scotland has had less dramatic upheavals but the more placid emergence has much to teach, and the study of these towns will not only enable us to appreciate their merits but will also make us better prepared for tending their future. However, as the full implications of this approach become clear, they will show that in town-making extreme positions are untenable; neither total preservation nor total clearance in rebuilding is consistent with the techniques of natural growth and evolution which Sir Frank Mears likened to those of the gardener rather than the man with the bulldozer. As consideration of contemporary town planning is not the purpose of this book, the effect of changes currently in progress is only briefly referred to because they are living instances of the process needed to keep towns in tune with the needs of their inhabitants. The evidence of such change comes from the proposals for altering, building and rebuilding which authorities receive from all quarters. Sir Frank Mears declared that the initiators of these proposals were the real planners, because whether they were intending to add a garage or room to their house, build a new house or office or a factory, they were planning. So also were the entrepreneurs, the house builders, the various authorities or government departments: when they produced their new projects either to demolish, extend or rebuild, they were actively participating in changing towns. From these events, Mears noted how we could read the trends and reinforce any tempo of change, and so better equip ourselves for preparing for and guiding development while maintaining the traditions of our Scottish planned towns.

1 Scotland up to 1100: the Historical Setting

The story of Scotland's towns should begin in the centuries before 1100. At the time of the Roman invasion the country consisted of minor kingdoms which had centres based on forts surrounded by small buildings, presumably houses, cattle sheds and workshops. Traprain Law and Eildon Hill North were notable examples. Evidence at the latter site indicates that its settlement was not laid out on a geometrical framework, although defence systems were constructed. The buildings were placed at random positions presumably selected merely for the practical availability of each individual plot for building. There have been reservations in describing such settlements as towns, but with large numbers – probably as many as 2,000 – living close together, the assumed degree of central direction and mutual co-operation suggests sufficient organisation to justify the appellation of a town. Later, small settlements developed at the focus of cross-country routes, river crossings or landing places for boats. Analysis of the burghs planned after 1100 reveals that many of these earlier small settlements were incorporated in the plans, as at Perth, Stirling, Edinburgh, Dumfries and elsewhere. A third possible generator of towns were the early church foundations, especially at St Andrews, Glasgow and Whithorn and Abernethy(1).

1 Abernethy. The remains of one of the most ancient settlements in Scotland may lie beneath this small town, with its market cross, early Christian tower and eighteenth-century and nineteenth-century houses.

If the estimates of several hundred thousand which have been made of Scotland's population in 1100 are correct, most people belonged to farming families living in very small groups in the Lowlands and coastal strips and moving about during the year to favourable summer grazings. The Highland forests would be left unpeopled for the bear, lynx and wolf to roam and, in the north, for herds of elk. Facts about the towns up to this date will remain meagre until archaeology uncovers more evidence.

After 1100 the story becomes clearer. From the accession of David I in 1124 there began in Scotland the most complete scheme of co-ordinated national, regional and town planning that Britain has ever seen. It continued for nearly 160 years until the death in 1286 of Alexander III, the last of the Canmore dynasty. David found his kingdom to be multi-lingual, for Gaelic was widely spoken, as well as the form of English called Scots used south of the Forth. Furthermore, many dialects existed, nearly unintelligible to people from outwith the areas where they were spoken, and so travel was inhibited. The Celtic church, renowned for its scholarship, was almost devoid of national organisation. The people conducted a primitive form of trade by barter. Communication relied on tidal rivers and the sea. All this occurred at the time when the Lowlands had become a unified constitution in a fragile state of potential insecurity, and Moray had still to be subdued to make the kingdom safe.

The Normans had conquered England two generations earlier and had earned high reputation for their efficiency and power. This Viking progeny, whose forebears had terrorised the Scots, blossomed into civilised Frenchmen retaining the Viking drive, discipline, brains and flair for success. Their war strategy and social organisation were recognised as beyond compare in Europe. They introduced the feudal system to England with trial by jury and standards of luxury and administrative efficiency hitherto unknown there. However, in Scotland, Norman influence was slight.

David had been brought up among these men at the Anglo-Norman Court of Henry, who was called 'the Clerk' because of his insistence on having the affairs of State properly recorded. Henry had married Matilda, David's sister, and David himself, half English, became Baron of Cumbria. He associated with many of the Norman nobles, owners of ninety-nine percent of England, Norman scholars and churchmen. Amongst these Normans were to be found men from the Low Countries, especially Flemings, who appear to have established a reputation as urban specialists.

After the collapse of Rome, rebuilding in Europe did not recommence until the period covered by the tenth to the fourteenth centuries. In the south of France the great abbeys founded new towns, which they named Bastides; in the north similar new towns were called Bastilles. Royalty followed these examples and Louis VII, a contemporary of David I, began building Bastides in the west of France. Later Edward I of England continued the process in his French domains. All of these towns were planned on the square grid pattern of the Roman camp, which in turn had given form to the Roman colonial towns. Later, after David's time, Edward I expanded his new town building into Ireland and Wales specifically as colonial towns, designed to implant English colonies in these relatively foreign lands which the English had annexed.

The new town building which also proceeded apace in the eleventh century in the German States where Flemings had participated did not follow the style of the French and English models. As a result of his studies in the Low Countries, Sir Frank Mears believed that Flemish skill in this field resulted from their experience in the organisation of towns and town life in what is now Belgium and Flanders — a view which history confirms. The new burghs were derived from that source totally uninfluenced by the continental geometric gridiron types.

The National Plan

When David was confronted by the challenge of launching his new kingdom, he naturally sought the assistance of his Anglo-Norman (including Flemish) friends. He did not, however, call for slavish imitation of French or Norman practice. He had his own personal insights and the strength of authority to follow them without conflicting with the worthwhile experience of others. The results show him to have been an exceptionally able planner with a resourceful and original approach to the building of a kingdom. The king's plan comprised four elements: (**1**) the introduction of the feudal system; (**2**) the establishment and maintenance of law and order; (**3**) the reorganisation of the Church as the national vehicle for religion, culture, scholarship and science; (**4**) the promotion of local and foreign trade.

The Feudal System

The feudal system which David I introduced to Scotland differed from the rigid caste system which bound the Englishman and his lord. In formulating this first constituent of the National Plan, the king aimed to forge a chain of mutual responsibility throughout society. Hitherto, the Celtic parts of Scotland had been joined in a paternalistic clan system. David I showed his genius by accepting this into his policy. The result was that the lesser orders there pledged their loyalty not to a Norman incomer as in England, but to the Mormaer chief of known and respected lineage.

In England, practically the whole country was parcelled out to the foreign friends of the Conqueror. By contrast, not more than ten to twenty percent of Scotland went to Normans, Bretons, Flemings or Englishmen. In Celtic Scotland David established the Mormaers as his Earls. The Mormaers, the Celtic regional commanders-in-chief, became the Earls of Angus and Mearns, Atholl and Gowrie, Strathearn and Menteith, Fife, Mar and Buchan, Moray and Ross and Argyll, which last extended beyond the present county of that name.

The Earldom of Galloway departed from this arrangement. It bordered with the king's own English barony of Cumbria and followed closer to the English pattern. The king had given it to his friend Fergus — perhaps unwisely, for it was to prove a problem to subsequent rulers. One of Fergus's successors 'threw off the Yoke of Scotland', declaring his independence until subdued by royal arms. On another occasion when the people of Galloway appealed to Alexander II against the actions of their lord, the king refused to intervene, deeming this illegal. Galloway was to develop few burghs, and only Dumfries became a royal one. Fortunately for the stability of the nation, this province was exceptional.

Caithness also did not conform with the other parts of the country, but for different reasons. At this time it included Sutherland and was under the Norse Earls of Orkney, while the Bishopric of Orkney was under Hamburg, and bore no relationship to the Celtic church. Administratively, Caithness stood outside Scotland. By the time of Alexander II (1219–49) changes separated the Bishopric with its Cathedral at Dornoch from Orkney to St Andrews. The king exercised his powers to depose the Earl of Caithness for his bad treatment of the bishop. By 1330 the de Cheynes of Norman name occupied Auld Wick Castle near Wick, and possessed about a third of the county. Orkney became Scottish towards the end of the 13th century; Shetland remained under the Norse Earls of Orkney till 1195, when the islands were transferred to the direct rule of the Norwegian throne, and so remained for centuries.

The north-western isles were under Norse control until the defeat of Hacon at the battle of Largs in 1263, when they were sold to Scotland. Burghs as a consequence were not established on the isles during the Canmore period. It will be seen that for the effective introduction of feudalism, David I was limited to the lands of the Mormaers and the Angles. There, every man who did not already have a chief or superior had to attach himself to one.

This requirement did not apply to townsmen in the royal burghs, because they owed allegiance only to the king, and together with the sheriffs, they were an effective check on the power of the earls. The increase of feudalism in Scotland was benevolently applied, for although a serf was theoretically a slave of his feudal lord, owing service for his land and protection, freemen were known to have sold themselves into serfdom. On the other hand, any serf who could buy himself land in a burgh and hold it unchallenged for a year and a day was free. In practice, by the end of the thirteenth century the semi-servile class had greatly declined. They had imperceptibly passed into being freemen, as tenants, sub-tenants, or cottars paying rent but owing no service. The ecclesiastical landowners particularly fostered this emancipation.

Law and Order
The second component of the National Plan, the establishment and maintenance of law and order, applied essentially to the management of towns. It involved the erection of castles, preferably on a defensible site often influencing the selection of a town's location. Feudalism carried the inherent danger that an earl might be tempted to declare himself independent, as one of the Earls of Galloway did, thus setting himself above the law. The king effectively avoided this danger by separating the administration of law from the power of the earls. The latter were the 'lairds', not the police nor justiciary. He entrusted the maintenance of internal law and order to the sheriffs, who occupied castles throughout the land and kept local forces of men under arms to enforce law and order.

Twelfth-century and thirteenth-century sheriffs were stationed at the following places: Berwick; Roxburgh; Selkirk; Peebles; Haddington; Edinburgh; Linlithgow; Stirling; Clackmannan; Dunfermline, and other unnamed places in Fife; Perth; Scone; Forfar; Kincardine; Aberdeen; Banff; Elgin; Forres; Nairn; Inverness; Cromarty; Skye; Lorne and Kintyre; Dumbarton; Lanark; Ayr; Dumfries. The list may not be complete, but it demonstrates the spread of burghs in medieval times. Obvious gaps occur in the north (perhaps Dingwall and Dornoch) and the south-west (Rutherglen, Annan). Two matters, however, are clear. First, the sheriffs greatly exceeded the numbers of earls. Their territories were too restricted for them to cherish grand ideas of their might or independence. Conversely, any earl would have to meet the combined pressure of several local sheriffs and their men should he show intimations of self-aggrandisement. The royal statecraft was brilliant and without equal in England or most other countries.

It was exceptional for the sheriff not to have a castle attached to a burgh and occupied with royal consent by his right of office, not of ownership(2). This differed fundamentally from the English lord of the manor with his castle and town. The sheriff was responsible for training the townsmen as a force in arms to apprehend malefactors great or small. This force was that of freemen, loyal king's men, independent of any earl or other feudal superior.

2 Edinburgh: Edinburgh Castle, Baird's Close, Grassmarket. In the foreground, a few simple houses at a close at the end of the Grassmarket; in the background, the towering fortress, royal apartments and banqueting hall provide urban drama by maximum contrast.

Lawgiving finally lay in the hands of the king who administered the responsibility ably and justly. Although the burghs had their courts, and the King's Chamberlain kept a vigilant watch on their administration, the king himself travelled from burgh to burgh, holding courts and settling disputes.

It is said that most of the sheriffs of David I were Anglo-Normans counterbalancing the Mormaers and other native earls, and Norman law may have been adapted for Scotland to take account of local customs and procedures.

3 Edinburgh: Lawnmarket and High Street, early nineteenth century. Even as late as this period the Lawnmarket preserved the tradition of an open market selling fabrics and fine lawns and linens. There was no tourist traffic, and the George IV Bridge had yet to be built.

Churches and Monasteries

The third component of the king's plan was provided by the churches and monasteries. Many of the religious establishments having been built close to the towns to supply religious teaching and education, they enhanced the visual quality of the burghs by the fine architectural quality of their buildings(**3**).

Queen Margaret had begun the process of reforming church organisation, and David I was to accelerate it. While her brilliant warrior husband Malcolm was fighting his way to unify Scotland, Margaret set about bringing new culture and graces to the court and installing her particular practices of religion by introducing Norman clerics into Scotland.

The Celtic Church, often called the Culdees, was characteristically introverted and unorganised. Its bishops had no territories. Their duties were to ensure the apostolic succession for the consecration of the clergy. The outstanding men of the Culdees tended to be Abbots – chosen for their outstanding qualities, not for their ability to administrate. St Columba, one of their most distinguished men and Abbot of

Iona, never became a bishop. The Culdees were good, faithful missionaries but did little in the way of parish ministry. They had the tradition of hermits and scholars.

These circumstances arose partly because of their own Celtic temperament and partly as a result of the Anglo-Saxon invasions of England when they had been cut off from Rome and France — their main source of Christian organisation and development. Thus, the Celtic Church in Ireland and Scotland had progressed in its own way and by its own resources.

The coming of the Normans brought England back into the mainstream of Rome, with the Norman clerics showing the same organisational ability as their warrior kin. It was with them that David grew up.

Queen Margaret had Roman clergy as court chaplains, and she brought the first Benedictines to Scotland in 1070, founding a priory for them at Dunfermline. But she also endowed several of the foundations of the Celtic Church and out of piety visited its hermits.

Edgar and Alexander I behaved very much in the same way — there was little change in the ecclesiastical emphasis. A detail of interest, however, is that Alexander brought a new order of fine craftsmen monks (the Tironensians) direct from Tiron in France and established them with an abbey at Selkirk. Under David I they removed to Kelso.

It was David I who made the change as part of his National Plan. The church was essential in the advancement of his realm. It was to be responsible not only for religion, but also for scholarship, agricultural science, the arts and what would now be called the social services — mainly distribution of charity, and the administration of hostels, almshouses and hospitals. For the king, it was essential that this be organised to function flawlessly, but the Celtic Church was characteristically disorganised.

So David introduced the Roman orders throughout Scotland. They came from France as well as England, to erect their monasteries on the lands provided by the king. The austere Cistercians received good lands well away from the burghs, for they were the agricultural researchers of the time; but the preaching order, the Dominican friars, and the Augustinian canons had generally to be located close to the burghs. Because of that policy the Greyfriars' and Blackfriars' monasteries lay just beyond the walls of the towns, and so indicate in modern times the limits of medieval urban boundaries.

Before David's accession six or seven such foundations were made, but in his twenty-nine-year reign at least forty more were established. Although subsequent kings of the Canmore line added a further sixty-seven foundations, the most important began in King David's reign — including the abbeys of Dunfermline, Kelso, Holyrood, Melrose, Jedburgh,

Cambuskenneth, Newbattle, Dundrennan, Dryburgh, Saulseat, Kilwinning, Paisley and Coupar Angus. Many of these became mother houses to which other foundations were attached.

Alexander II, in his thirty-year reign from 1219–49, founded further abbeys less powerful than those already established, such as Culross, Tongland, Deer, Inchcolm, Holywood, Balmerino, Aberdeen and Fearn.

David I also endowed bishoprics at Glasgow, Dunblane, Aberdeen, Ross (Fortrose) and possibly in theory rather than fact, one at Dornoch for Caithness; but the most important was St Andrews, for it soon became the Metropolitan Bishopric, the seat of the Scottish Archbishop. The king recognised its status because within three years from the start of his reign he linked to this bishopric the right to have a burgh, in all respects similar to his own royal burghs, except that the superior was the bishop, not the king. And with the charter he introduced the man to bring it to fruition, Mainard 'the Fleming' (though the name was Norman) 'the King's own Burgess in Berwick-on-Tweed'. He was called the Prepositus.

In similar manner a burghal charter was given to the Bishop of Glasgow, and his town was laid out by Randolf of Haddington, a Norman. And another was given to the Abbot of Holyrood, which resulted in the separate Burgh of Canongate beside the Royal Burgh of Edinburgh. In St Andrews and Glasgow, the castles were occupied by the bishops, not sheriffs.

The Celtic monks were welcomed into the Roman orders, and many became members of the new houses. But those who could not bring themselves to do so were allowed to continue. Thus St Mary's on the Rock at St Andrews remained as the Culdee Church beside the Cathedral, and inexplicably, apart from their scholarship the Culdee monks tended to become the civil servants of their day.

Local and Foreign Trade

To achieve the fourth objective, the promotion of trade, the planning of a network of towns became vital. David I and his successors up to the end of the thirteenth century applied themselves to this enterprise with masterly effect. They distributed the new chartered towns in locations over the whole part of the country where agriculture was practicable, so that the benefit of the plan would reach all the king's subjects, not just those living in Scotland's south-east. These royal burghs, totalling thirty-one, were: Berwick; Roxburgh; Jedburgh; Peebles; Haddington; Edinburgh; Linlithgow; Stirling; Inverkeithing; Dunfermline; Kinghorn; Kirkcaldy; Crail; Perth; Forfar; Montrose; Aberdeen; Fyvie; Elgin; Forres; Nairn; Inverness; Cromarty; Dingwall; Dumbarton; Lanark; Renfrew; Irvine; Ayr; Wigtown; and Dumfries.

Similar trading rights applied to the towns of the bishops of St Andrews, Glasgow and Brechin – although the latter town did not enjoy the title of burgh. Besides these about eight other towns were founded without being royal burghs. A royal burgh was given the exclusive trading rights of its sheriffdom. Goods for sale had to be offered in the burgh market and toll paid thereon. These dues were levied in several ways, one being on entry at the town gate, hence the requirement that towns had to be enclosed. Charges were also made for the letting of stalls on each market day – one halfpence if the booth was covered and one farthing if uncovered. The sale of food was less tightly restricted than other goods: it could be bought anywhere and sold in any burgh market after toll had been paid. Its price, along with that of ale, was fixed by the market authorities, and any attempt at hoarding for resale was treated as an offence. In these days of difficult travel, this easing of trade boundaries on food stuffs meant more than it would now. All perishables had to be sold quickly, usually at the nearest market, and long distances for transport in warm weather would have prevented the delivery of fresh supplies. Even in those days a man's pint was the subject of the Revenue's grasping attention. The burgh brewer was taxed four pence per year – very little, but the principle had been established.

The burghs, in spite of their mercantile activities, were very much agricultural communities, owning lands outside the town. At Ayr for instance each burgess who occupied a toft (a plot in the town of under a quarter of an acre) had an entitlement of six acres of cleared land outside the burgh as well as a share in the common grazings. So there was a degree of self-support with which the countryman had to compete if he brought his produce for sale to the market.

The sale of other goods was strictly controlled. Manufacturers had to present their goods for sale at their local markets, although most of the craftsmen dwelt in the burghs. Export and import business was confined to members of the merchant class.

The manufactures consisted chiefly of cloth, wood, leather, fireclay or iron artifacts. The country folk and some poorer people in the burghs wore garments of rough white or grey woolen material. The finished, dyed cloth produced for the garb of the well-to-do was the monopoly of the burgesses, that is, the merchants. Iron ore, not yet mined or smelted in Scotland, was imported in bars and wrought by the smiths. Local leather, notoriously poor owing to lack of knowledge or skill in tanning, provided the material for shoes or, with the hair on, coats. The well-tanned foreign leather imported by the merchants was used initially for making shields and household utensils until superseded by iron. The skill of the local carpenters ensured that better houses and buildings with wood framing served the southern burghs. In addition to the imports already described, the merchants brought in dyes, thread, beeswax, soap, wines and spices of all sorts to make palatable the salt-meat in winter.

Exports included wood, hides and furry skins, salmon, herring and wool – the last from the Borders and Moray mainly, through Berwick and Aberdeen. This export-import trade, though small, revitalised the life of the new nation. It opened new horizons of great riches to many, and bore risk to the ruin of others.

The establishment of more burghs and the creation of burgesses

These early burghs succeeded so notably that it became every noble's ambition to have one, and a second class of burghs grew up. Their progress varied. Many were probably initiated not as part of a co-ordinated plan but more as a means of bolstering the prestige of a feudal lord, or through speculative enterprise to augment his purse. Sometimes the right to have a burgh was granted by the king in genuine gratitude for services rendered. At others, the sovereign may have felt it politic to recognise the importance of his vassal by the right to have a burgh. William the Lion tended to be less discriminating in granting burghal charters, although in some instances he merely confirmed earlier recognitions. By the end of the Canmore period there were arguably too many burghs – leading to friction between them.

The system of self-government which was to evolve in the centuries that followed the establishment of the burghs grew from the organisation that David I implanted as part of his National Plan. First he distinguished the leading townspeople as burgesses. These burgesses, men and women, were divided into merchants and craftsmen. But not all merchants were members of the merchants' guild: humble packmen could be merchants but not guild members. The right to have a merchants' guild was as specific as that to have a burgh, although not all towns had a guild or wanted one. Merchants' guilds generally belong to the latter part of the medieval period, while the similar foundation of crafts' guilds did not take place till beyond that time. There is uncertainty as to the precise function of the merchants' guilds when first constituted. References show that in some cases most townsmen and many craftsmen received permission to join these guilds, so that a guild could claim to speak for the burgh. On the other hand, behaviour on the part of the guilds tended to emphasise their sense of being a powerful élite who took seriously their responsibilities in relation both to their own trading interests and to the wider interests of their towns. They arranged reciprocal trading rights with the guilds of other burghs and organised social welfare within their own.

Burgesses were sharply divided from the rest of the town's

4 Edinburgh: Dewar's Close, Grassmarket. Excessive overcrowding created this dark, fearsome alley out of which one escaped by a steep flight of stairs to the summit and daylight.

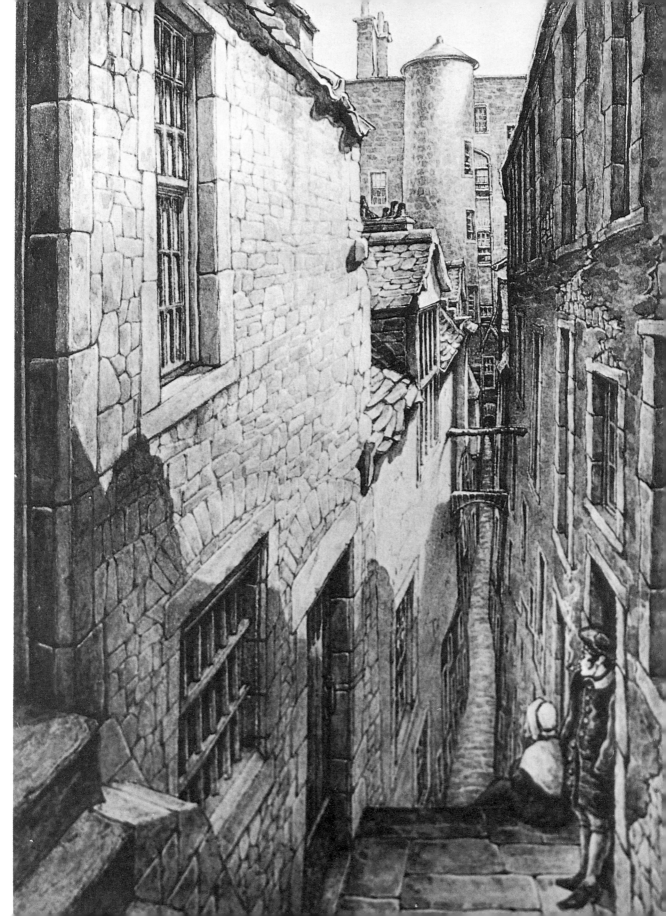

population – servants, apprentices, dependents, the jobless and the unfit. A burgess had to own a toft in the burgh. He occupied it rent-free till he built his house within a limited time prescribed by the king. In some burghs the time was one year. Exceptions were Dumbarton, where a period of five years operated, and Dingwall, where the limit was ten years. This could be seen as an early case of differential inducement to aid dispersal of population.

A burgess who inherited his land could leave it only to his heirs, or give them the first offer if he elected to sell it. He might divide his land amongst his family as he pleased. These two provisions were important. The first limited the opportunity for serfs to become free. The king's laws provided for any serf to buy a toft in a burgh and hold it unchallenged for a year and a day and thus become free, but infrequent availability could have partially frustrated this procedure. The hereditary rights to land did not altogether ensure the status of members of the family, for sons of merchants remained freemen (and most merchants were burgesses) only so long as their father lived – unless they at the time had also become merchants.

The second procedure is important and had significant implications for the future of burghs, for it led to the sub-division of tofts, and much later in some places (notably Edinburgh) to overcrowding(**4**).

The Burgh Courts

Questions of succession in the royal burghs were dealt with by the burgh courts, as also were the duties of 'watch and ward'. Every able-bodied burgess had to take his share of these police duties, and failure to do so, or to do it properly, led to punishment if he had not made alternative arrangements. A burgess could appeal from his own court to the Court of the Four Burghs, the burghs in question being Berwick, Roxburgh, Edinburgh and Stirling. These four had uniform laws which owed much to continental precedent, but especially to the laws of Newcastle-upon-Tyne. This uniformity was in marked contrast to the individuality of the laws of the English boroughs.

Uniformity in the application of law in the burghs may have resulted more from the annual inspection by the Burgh Chamberlain into the administration in the burgh than from specific codifying of law. The chamberlain's inspection, no sinecure, was most carefully carried out. He dealt firstly with the prefect or 'Prepositus', the link between the king and his burgesses. At times the Prepositus was 'given' by the King, like Mainard to St Andrews. At times he was nominated by the burgh and accepted by the crown. Often a burgh had two, and the Prepositus had baillies who worked for him. Otherwise the administration of the early burghs evolved from considerations of convenience, common sense and impartiality, with latterly the merchant guild playing an influential or dominant part, and the principal burgesses accepting a share of all responsibilities. Only later did specific organisations become distinct within each burgh and between the burghs, particularly royal burghs, who formed their Convention. Thus, while the chamberlain's inspection began with the Prepositus and baillies, it could, and often did lead him to hear the humblest burgess. The townsmen of the bishops' and barons' burghs did not have this close access to the crown as of right, and there was nothing approaching this close relationship in England.

2 National Planning: David I (1124-53)

The burgh plans

Every Scottish town has a High Street. It may not always be named that, but the long single streets that have provided the back bone of urban life for centuries possess qualities that distinguish them from the streets in the rest of the towns. Many extend to about 400 yards (366 metres) in length, some remain under 200 yards (183 metres), and others reach to about half a mile (0.8 kilometres). The heightened animation of the unfolding prospect obtained from walking along these streets derives from the slight curve of the frontages which close off the distant end of the street while bringing ever more of the fronts of the buildings into view the further one progresses(5).

These curving fronts are not parallel. The street usually widens gradually to half way along the length and then gently returns to its narrower width; or it may widen from one end to its widest at the other like an elongated triangle(6). Some have more than one widened portion along the full length.

Few High Streets run level over their whole lengths, and several lie on appreciable slopes. Narrow lanes, obviously of some antiquity, which lead at right angles from the streets, mostly run downhill(7). The fronts of the buildings along the streets frequently extend to no more than about 22 feet (6.7 metres) and wide façades consist apparently of multiples of this minimum dimension(8). Usually the High Street contains the parish church and graveyard, the tolbooth and market cross. Castles or their ruins may lie close by, and minor roads nearly parallel flank one or both sides at a distance of about 100 yards (91.4 metres) or more from the street frontages.

As has been indicated, these qualities, so vital to the character of the older Scottish towns, were determined from as far back as the twelfth century, when the country lay remote from Rome, the centre of medieval culture, and its church affairs were simple, its trade and mercantile performance poor. Central authority was established but not effectively exercised. To solve these problems the country needed the application of a single energetic, far-ranging, practical and dedicated mind. This David I grasped so that he controlled the nobles and consolidated his rule firmly but reasonably peacefully. He founded the many important abbeys and religious houses from his own purse on land which he provided. In matters pertaining to prosperity in trade and urban development, he excelled.

The king quickly perceived that to accomplish his plans he

5 Edinburgh: Lawnmarket and Castle Hill. The effectiveness of the gentle winding of an almost straight street is apparent. Gillespie-Graham's great steeple rises high above the frame of the photograph, while the Outlook Tower of Sir Patrick Geddes and the Castle form arresting climaxes to the composition of the street.

18

6 Selkirk: Market Place. The centre, based on a triangular-shaped plan, is complimented by the steeple and Town House (where Sir Walter Scott sat as Sheriff), the market cross, the eighteenth-century and ninteenth-century houses and the modern post office. The centre could achieve perfection if the pitched roof were restored to the eighteenth-century building next to the Town House, if the upper storey were built to fill in the gap to the right of the picture and if the roads were flagged and paved.

required money. He recognised the simple commercial truth which has been known equally throughout history from the pharoahs to Mr Marks or Mr Spencer – that to make money quickly one must buy at the lowest obtainable cost and sell at the highest acceptable price. The king, however, applied this axiom in a way less direct – as befitted his position. His plan was to create the conditions for trade where others could operate, and he would then collect revenue by way of rents and taxes. This

7 Edinburgh: Fountain Close, High Street, 1833. This close emphasises the Scottish conception that town buildings are the enclosing elements in an outdoor space. Here, as in a tree-lined avenue, they even branch inwards to give shelter from rain and wind.

required bodies of able merchants and traders, and it needed places for them to live and traffic.

The first royal towns

The towns that existed in Scotland when David's reign began would not have been planned to meet the needs of merchants. Edinburgh Castle, for example, would have attracted a minor settlement of adherents or servants ranged along the narrow road leading up to the open defence zone, now the Esplanade. This road on the line of Castle Hill would be joined by the road leading round the south side of the Nor' Loch and up the slopes above to enter Castle Hill at what is now known as Ramsay Lane(**I**). The routes from the west and the south would join below the ridge and mount up hill by way of a path close to the Bow, up to the foot of Castle Hill. Similarly, Stirling, Linlithgow and Perth were restricted to a few houses grouped near castle or palace, or along the waterside as at Perth, where at the fordable point major routes would focus. None, however, had then adequate space or accommodation to provide what the king had

8 Berwick-on-Tweed. The elimination of vehicles in this attractive centre, together with a well devised scheme of paving, would raise the street to the top rank of town design and planning.

21

in mind. David selected each of them, however, to be royal burghs and set out new market streets or places, so initiating Scotland's first new towns. Others such as Rutherglen, Elgin(**II**), Forres(**III**), Berwick and Peebles may also have had early beginnings of growth associated with castles, and they were created royal burghs along with Roxburgh, Dunfermline, Montrose(**IV**) and Aberdeen. In the twenty-nine years of David's rule up to 1153, thirteen new royal towns were established with four others under the royal authority, by bishops at Canongate and St Andrews, and by nobles at Haddington and Renfrew.

Map I Edinburgh, twelfth–thirteenth century. A typical twelfth-century plan in the south of the country, running east–west with the market area as shown about 20 feet (6 metres) wider than today. The Grassmarket was introduced later in the century because of the early success of the burgh.

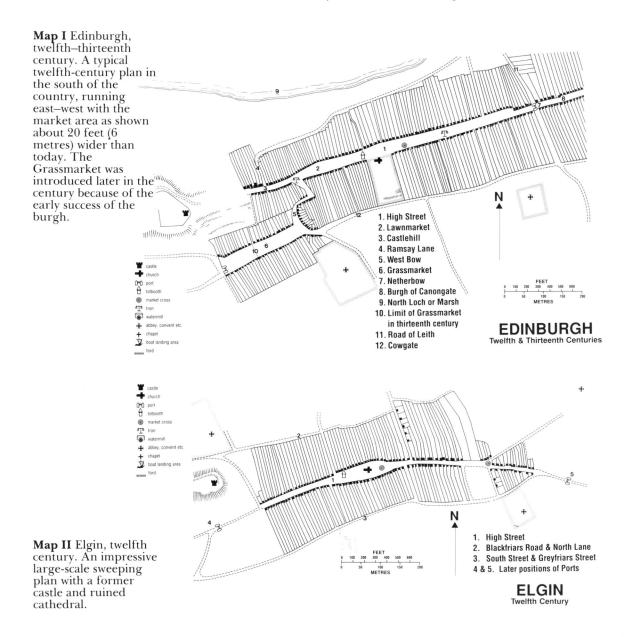

1. High Street
2. Lawnmarket
3. Castlehill
4. Ramsay Lane
5. West Bow
6. Grassmarket
7. Netherbow
8. Burgh of Canongate
9. North Loch or Marsh
10. Limit of Grassmarket in thirteenth century
11. Road of Leith
12. Cowgate

EDINBURGH
Twelfth & Thirteenth Centuries

castle
church
port
tolbooth
market cross
tron
watermill
abbey, convent etc.
chapel
boat landing area
ford

ELGIN
Twelfth Century

1. High Street
2. Blackfriars Road & North Lane
3. South Street & Greyfriars Street
4 & 5. Later positions of Ports

Map II Elgin, twelfth century. An impressive large-scale sweeping plan with a former castle and ruined cathedral.

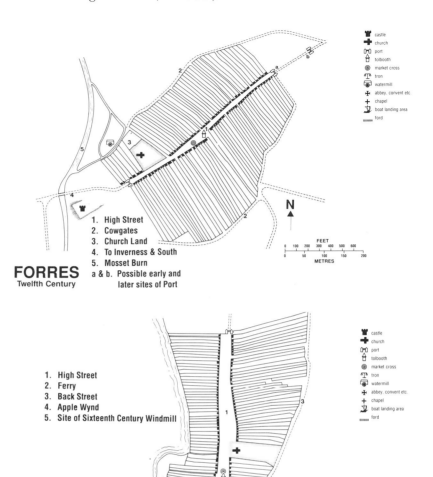

Map III Forres, twelfth century. The burgh has a well preserved twelfth-century plan which can still be distinguished on the site.

castle
church
port
tolbooth
market cross
tron
watermill
abbey, convent etc.
chapel
boat landing area
ford

1. High Street
2. Cowgates
3. Church Land
4. To Inverness & South
5. Mosset Burn
a & b. Possible early and later sites of Port

N

FEET
0 100 200 300 400 500 600
0 50 100 150 200
METRES

FORRES
Twelfth Century

1. High Street
2. Ferry
3. Back Street
4. Apple Wynd
5. Site of Sixteenth Century Windmill

castle
church
port
tolbooth
market cross
tron
watermill
abbey, convent etc.
chapel
boat landing area
ford

N

Map IV Montrose, twelfth century. A beautifully situated planned town. As in many other burghs, High Street was slightly narrowed after the medieval period but still has a spacious quality.

FEET
0 100 200 300 400 500 600
0 50 100 150 200
METRES

MONTROSE
Twelfth Century

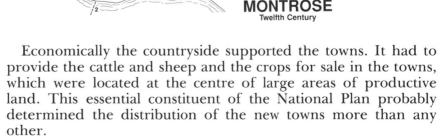

Economically the countryside supported the towns. It had to provide the cattle and sheep and the crops for sale in the towns, which were located at the centre of large areas of productive land. This essential constituent of the National Plan probably determined the distribution of the new towns more than any other.

Accessibility from existing routes would also be taken into account in the choice of sites, but when a town began to function

9 Edinburgh: the Little Mound, early nineteenth century. All the medieval rigs or gardens have been filled with the great lands of flatted houses, leaving only the narrow closes leading down from the Royal Mile. The new Bank of Scotland is prominent. In the foreground is a bleachfield for linen.

the countryman would beat a path to its ports or gates if no route had existed before.

The national strategy provided the wide-angled, soft-edge view of where new towns were needed. Other factors pinpointed sites in sharp focus. For example, in areas in the north of Midlothian several sites would seem to have been possible. Musselburgh and Leith had advantages in their access to sea traffic on the River Esk and the Water of Leith and possessed abundant land for building and cultivation. Dalkeith was located on a site which lay at the junction of routes from the south, and had a defensible site for a castle near at hand, probably at the time already occupied. Nevertheless a steep site, with difficult access, uneconomic to build on and inconveniently located in relation to the townsmen's cultivation of rigs and meadows was selected for Edinburgh because of its formidable rock and fort(**9**). Stirling, similarly handicapped as a town location, gained preference over other possible sites because of its powerful stronghold. Linlithgow had the advantage of a good defensible site on the loch for the castle and palace. St Andrews possessed a defensible site for a castle and was a long-standing religious centre. Haddington and Perth were exceptions because they did not possess natural strong points and had to build forts without such advantage. Free from the topographical restrictions of other towns, Haddington was planned on more spacious and imaginative lines(**10**). Set back from its castle and church, St Andrews also achieved one of the most noble town plans in Britain(**11**).

The castles were regarded as essential elements in national defence. They also provided bases for the king or his chamberlain as he moved about administering government affairs — a mode of administration which contrasts with the

10 Haddington. The great expanse of the twelfth-century triangular planned market-place may be appreciated from this view. Clearly shown are the later main central encroachment with the Burgh Chambers, classical steeple and two smaller infills at each end. Some of the long rigs of the burgesses' houses may also be distinguished.

11 St Andrews. This impressive plan, with its three principal streets converging on the abbey, has evolved from the twelfth century by the exercise of wise planning. Despite periods of regression and decay, the plan is one of the finest in the country.

centralised, long-distance control preferred by the modern London business oligarchies.

When the sites were selected the lay-out of the towns could proceed. Of first importance and at the centre was the market. The area had to serve all aspects of the merchants' business. Each Fair Day sheep and cattle were brought in along with wool, fleeces, hides, cloth, grain and fish – as well as the products of the craftsmen, souters, lorimers, baxters, brewsters, fabers, cordiners and others. Room had to be set aside for the fleshers, who slaughtered and prepared the meat carcases, and for the tanners and skinners. Booths had to be set up for sellers and officials. All the first towns with the exception of Canongate were therefore a form of medieval supermarket, a vulgar commercial fact from which some refined conservationists will recoil.

Edinburgh

The natural features of the selected sites influenced the shapes of the towns. The long, relatively narrow ridge top of Edinburgh suited the long market-place, lying on an east-west axis of about half a mile (0.8 kilometres) (**I**, p.22). Originally, its width was about 100 feet (30.48 metres). The sides of the market would have been set off at equal distances from the path that would by then have been well established, running along the top of the ridge – the driest part, and possibly by-passing any rocky irregularity on the way. This natural line would not be exactly straight, and so the market would also deviate to the same degree. The widening from Castle Hill to Lawnmarket was effected gradually and not by forming an abrupt set-back in the frontages(**5**). Narrowing at the foot of High Street did not occur because the setting out of the separate burgh of Canongate in continuation did not call for narrowing. The narrow entrance, familiar in medieval town plans, was introduced to achieve the minimum width at the port for greater security and ease of controlling entry to the market-place. Although some cobbles would likely be laid to protect the surface of the area set aside for the fleshmarket or at the Cross where many people congregated, and at the narrow intensively traversed entrances to the ports, the markets were initially grassed. For this reason surface drainage would not constitute a problem, although some ditches may have been used at the sides of the market and between the tofts, that is, house plots. These tofts were set out at about right angles to the edge of the market-place. Their widths remain problematical. Some plots may have been made wider than others. Evidence in Lawnmarket in Edinburgh suggests an average of about 22 feet 4 inches (30 links; 6.76 metres), with some wider. In Stirling's Broad Street the average is about identical, and as in Edinburgh widths in the nineteenth century varied from 20 feet (6.09 metres) to 28 feet 6 inches (8.68 metres). Towns such as Linlithgow, Haddington and Elgin conform to these dimensions, but parts of Perth with shorter plots may have been wider: 30 feet to nearly 33 feet (40–45 links approximately; 9.14–10.58 metres).

The length of tofts varied considerably in individual towns because at the foot of the toft a service lane (cowgate) usually ran roughly parallel with the market street but often took an elliptical direction towards the entrance to the market at one or both ends, thus progressively shortening the plot lengths. This diversion partly served for the convenience of those using the lane and partly to relieve any occupier at the end of the lane from the unfair responsibility for and expense of erecting a long external palisade at the side and back to protect his land and the town in general. A good average length among larger plots was 400 feet (129.92 metres), and an average of 240 feet (73.15 metres) for the shorter lengths. At these dimensions a toft would fall well short of one square rood in area (13,725 square feet; 1275 square metres) which was prescribed in the laws of the burgh.

St Andrews

The lay-outs of towns at this period testify that medieval Scotland did not favour squares or wide rectangles for market-places. They also provide some variations from the typical expanding and contracting linear High Streets, and explanations of the various forms have not in every case been produced. St Andrews in particular has engendered conflicting theories among the experts(**V**). Some light may be thrown on the problem by considering the roads, for while buildings come and go in history, road lines survive.

First there was the religious centre of the eighth century which grew in importance up to the tenth century. This shrine with its holy relics drew pilgrims from far and near who, as they approached the church – probably on the site of St Mary's – would follow one of two routes. Those from the north would follow an uphill track on the line of North Street until they reached the top of the slope at the point where Union Street lies and then, turning slightly, would walk straight towards the church building. Those from the west and south would turn and follow the line of South Street until they reached the top of the path at about the point where Church Street lies, and then make straight down to the church. Thus, for over 200 years the tread of pilgrims' feet would have beaten out two well-defined tracks before St Andrews medieval town was built. Meanwhile, as in other towns, some building of dwellings for those associated with the church, and possibly the castle, would have gradually developed. As others have suggested in the past, Castle Street

Map V St Andrews, twelfth century. The town was planned in the twelfth century, and the growth of the burgh was guided by a perfect sense of urbanculture, making St Andrews one of the most distinguished plans in Britain.

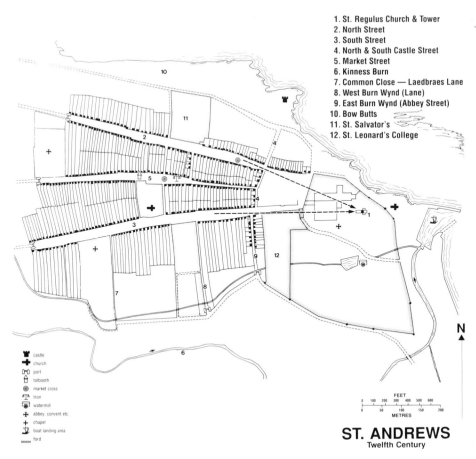

1. St. Regulus Church & Tower
2. North Street
3. South Street
4. North & South Castle Street
5. Market Street
6. Kinness Burn
7. Common Close — Laedbraes Lane
8. West Burn Wynd (Lane)
9. East Burn Wynd (Abbey Street)
10. Bow Butts
11. St. Salvator's
12. St. Leonard's College

castle
church
port
tolbooth
market cross
tron
watermill
abbey, convent etc.
chapel
boat landing area
ford

N

FEET
0 100 200 300 400 500 600
0   50   100   150   200
METRES

ST. ANDREWS
Twelfth Century

seems a possible location for the dwellings of these first inhabitants. Also, as usually happens at coastal towns, a fishermen's village would have been set up at a good landing place nearly at the mouth of the burn below the church.

Large numbers of pilgrims require space to congregate before a religious centre, as is demonstrated at the great churches in continental Europe. So one may infer that an open area between the precincts of the church and these first dwellings would have been set aside for stalls, packmen, hawkers and entertainers who would flock to the site at the time of religious festivals to sell drink, food, trinkets, toys, religious tokens and so on, adding to the throng of the locals and pilgrims. This area would have lain between the limits of North and South Street, and east of the backs of the dwellings.

Some buildings in the eleventh and twelfth centuries may have crept along North and South Streets, but when a new market street was needed in the twelfth century, it was laid out strictly in accordance with medieval planning principles. It occupied the ridge of the mound which rises from the south at the Kinness

Burn to the top at the centre and falls back to the north towards the coast line.

The top of the new street followed the line running east to west – nearly, as it happened, equally distant from the routes established on North Street and South Street. At its east end the new street would have been cut through between the plots on the west side of South Castle Street, and after clearing the then existing plots, would have widened out in the familiar way near Baker's Lane.

At the west end the new market would narrow again, and although building possibly terminated short of the modern Greyfriars' Garden, the route would continue westward, eventually to turn south to join with the existing track at South Street. The plots in Market Street would extend back to the tracks at South Street and North Street except at the east end, where some existing plots in North Street and perhaps South Street would curtail the depth. At the west end beyond the church the plots may have been planned to the full length available, about 450 feet (137 metres), but further plans for extending the town eventually reduced these plots to about half their depths.

The lands beyond South Street and North Street were likely to have remained as burgh rigs under cultivation in the twelfth century, and the common grazing meadows would lie still further beyond along the back of the Kinness Burn, reached by Common Close (Ladebraes Lane) West Burn Wynd (Lane) and Eastburn Wynd (Abbey Street). The planning of the plots at North Street and South Street would have been begun in the thirteenth century.

Perth

The plan of the Royal Burgh of Perth in the twelfth century has some similarity to St Andrews(**VI**). The first community lived along the waterfront where a quay or facility for beaching boats was available. A passage between led to the ford across the Tay (at the end of the century to be replaced by a bridge) via Stanners Island to the opposite shore where two routes followed up the bank, one north to Scone, the other south and turning east to Dundee. A few houses would have been placed on this other side to give shelter to travellers when crossing to Perth was delayed by flood. Also, the ford-woman would live there to carry travellers across, confirming the feminine suspicion that in early society women were ordained to be mankind's beasts of burden. This first settlement would consist of the Water Gate running south from a point perhaps just north of the ford, and a bow shot from the castle on the north east of the Castle Gable, and may have extended to Canal Street. The church was set back from the frontage at Water Gate in similar fashion to St

Map VI Perth, twelfth–thirteenth century. The royal burgh at High Street was planned in the twelfth century and followed by the parallel extension at South Street, after which a strong wall was erected with a broad ditch. The resulting square shape led some eighteenth-century antiquarians to speculate that the plan was Roman.

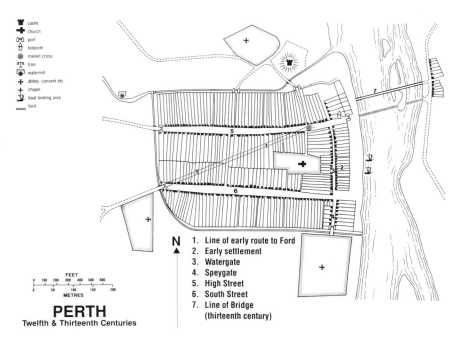

castle
church
port
tolbooth
market cross
tron
watermill
abbey, convent etc
chapel
boat landing area
ford

N

1. Line of early route to Ford
2. Early settlement
3. Watergate
4. Speygate
5. High Street
6. South Street
7. Line of Bridge
   (thirteenth century)

FEET
0 100 200 300 400 500 600
0   50   100   150   200
METRES

PERTH
Twelfth & Thirteenth Centuries

Andrews' parish church.

The problems emerge in following the sequence of the twelfth century extensions. It seems certain that High Street formed the first town which became King David's town, with its widened market area originally wider than the present street by probably 5–10 feet (1.5–3.0 metres). To occupy this position the road from the west would have had to be diverted, an inference now generally accepted. The depth of the plots on the south side may have been originally about equal to those on the north side, 145 feet (44.2 metres). The introduction of South Street seems to have followed on very rapidly in the twelfth century and left no time for a back lane to become established behind the yard heads of the plots on the south side of High Street. South Street's position may have been chosen to join the junction of existing routes leading to the town from the west and north-west (the Sheriffdom of Auchterarder). If these conjectures are accepted, the difference of depths of plots on either side of South Street would be explained. The water channel down Mill Street to provide a ditch to the castle was probably made at the time High Street was formed, but that at Canal Street may have been a later work undertaken after South Street was formed. However, South Street seems to have been the first planned extension made to a Scottish burgh.

Haddington
At Haddington the plan departed from the pronounced lineal form to a longer triangle: at its widest it approached nearly 300

feet (91.4 metres) as against 100 feet (30.48 metres) in Edinburgh(**VII**). As a result, the market area (5.8 acres; 2.35 hectares) enclosed in this much shorter town nevertheless exceeded that of Edinburgh (4.9 acres; 1.98 hectares).

As Haddington was for a time a royal town centred in a wide agricultural area with a number of small settled hamlets in the vicinity, a large market was probably regarded as necessary to handle flocks of sheep and cattle as well as to serve for the marketing of other produce. This does not explain why the shape differed from most of the contemporary towns which conformed to the linear shape, especially as the topography would permit a linear town if the planners of Haddington had preferred that. The fact that triangular market places and village greens do appear more frequently in England suggests that Anglo-Norman presence in East Lothian probably influenced those responsible for Haddington's lay-out.

The early settlements at Dalkeith and Selkirk also adopted triangular plans. Haddington had been assigned a royal residence off its market-place, and a castle may also have been erected, but no trace of it has yet been discovered.

Stirling

The first dwellings at Stirling may have been positioned at the site of the wooden bridge, but some building would likely have

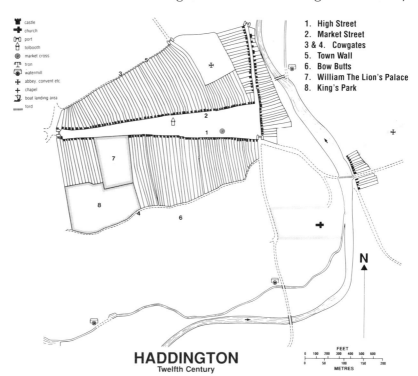

castle
church
port
tolbooth
market cross
tron
watermill
abbey, convent etc.
chapel
boat landing area
ford

1. High Street
2. Market Street
3 & 4. Cowgates
5. Town Wall
6. Bow Butts
7. William The Lion's Palace
8. King's Park

N

Map VII Haddington, twelfth century. The burgh was planned in the twelfth century on a scale appropriate to the countryside, which had rich agricultural land and was well populated.

HADDINGTON
Twelfth Century

FEET
0 100 200 300 400 500 600
0   50   100   150   200
METRES

Map VIII Stirling, twelfth–thirteenth century. In the twelfth century Stirling, like Edinburgh, was planned close to a castle and royal palace, but on a much smaller scale. It was later extended down Baker Street and Spittal Street.

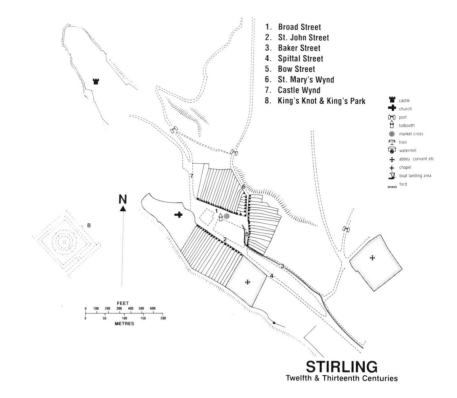

1. Broad Street
2. St. John Street
3. Baker Street
4. Spittal Street
5. Bow Street
6. St. Mary's Wynd
7. Castle Wynd
8. King's Knot & King's Park

castle
church
port
tolbooth
market cross
tron
watermill
abbey, convent etc
chapel
boat landing area
ford

N

FEET
0 100 200 300 400 500 600
0   50   100   150   200
METRES

STIRLING
Twelfth & Thirteenth Centuries

started near the early castle at the top of Castle Hill or Wynd. The difficulty occurs when the site of the twelfth-century royal town is considered(**VIII**). One suggestion sees the market extending across from the north side of Broad Street to the south frontage of St John Street, and extending from Mar's Wark to Bow Street. This would have given a market area of about 2.84 acres (1.15 hectares), only about half of the area in Edinburgh's Lawnmarket and High Street but ample for the need of a town where status derived from battlements rather than business. However, a stream is known to have followed down in a south-easterly direction from the south-east corner of this possible market area. The bank on the south side would likely have been relatively high at the top of what became Spittal Street, to the extent that the bridge which was built over the stream to give access to the south side of the market would be appreciably below the level of what is now St John Street (formerly Back Street). These factors suggest that the way up the ridge to the castle before the town was built was by way of a high road. The approach along King Street is directed straight to the castle on the hill, but Spittal Street (formerly Quality Street and High Gait) takes a direction slightly to the south, but would have been dry and provided a steady incline on the line of St John Street, Castle Wynd and the road up to the castle. On that basis St Mary's Wynd and later Baker Street would follow the building

12 Stirling: Broad Street. The wide market-place rises comfortably on the sloping way up to the castle. Its buildings still conform generally to the controlling widths of the original buildings which lined the street in medieval times. The tolbooth tower on the opposite frontage and the market cross also contribute to the character of the street.

of the market area with the stream adjusted to run down the side of the route on Baker Street.

The alternative theory is that Broad Street was the original market area with St John Street forming the Back Street on the south, and St Mary's Wynd performing a similar function on the north(**12**). On that basis the market area would have been restricted to less than three-quarters of an acre (0.305 hectares) – a size inadequate for a royal town, even allowing for the modest marketing activities. Expansion would have then been a necessity, and in size and shape the area embracing Baker Street and Spittal Street would seem to fit exactly these requirements, except that the cross-fall would impede the full use of the area as a market-place(**13**).

Until such time as archaeological evidence is produced to clarify the question, the larger market area would seem better fitted for meeting the requirement of a royal town – to create an attractive market to bring in worthwhile revenues to the king. Accepting this theory, the Tolbooth and other buildings on the south side of Broad Street became a late medieval infilling of the market-place, as is found in Haddington, Elgin and other towns.

Rutherglen

The remaining royal towns of David's reign were planned in the typical medieval fashion of the time, except for Rutherglen. It has two eccentricities which distinguish it from its contemporaries. Main Street (the market) narrows at the centre of its length, and the plots to the north have little depth (average 110 feet, 33.5 metres) while those to the south are at least 400 feet (122 metres) and increase to about 500 feet (150 metres). The reverse narrowing may have resulted from an initial plan confining the town to a market beginning at the church, where

13 Stirling: Spittal Street and Bow Street. Glengarry Lodge, a sixteenth-century house in Spittal Street, and the adjacent Spittal's House are well sited and frame the way up Bow Street on the left. The two large houses in Bow Street, Darnley House and Moir-of-Leckie's House (at the back), date partly from the seventeenth century but mostly from the eighteenth century. Bow Street, narrow and climbing, once made a dramatic entry into Broad Street, but it was widened in a straight line not very cleverly after the war.

the street is narrow, and widening eastward to terminate at Farmelown Road. The market on that basis would have embraced nearly 3 acres (1.214 hectares), adequate for the town's rural and local trade. The plots to the north of Main Street may have been curtailed by the closeness of the castle, which might have been positioned in the twelfth century at a distance of only 200 feet (61 metres) from the north side of the market at Castle Street. The route between Glasgow and the south-east to Lanark running south of the Clyde may have been diverted at the east Port into the town, which would explain the sharp turn northwards from the road as it approached the town from the south-east.

Aberdeen

The origin of Aberdeen had similarities to the sequence of growth later experienced by Glasgow. The difference lay in the complications of the changes experienced in Aberdeen. The oldest part of the town was positioned at the south-east and was called the Sea Town. This had a castle on the Castle Hill, and a market-place. William the Lion had built a palace there which was later gifted to the Trinity Friars, and the royal palace was donated to the Dominicans. This town was razed by Edward III in 1330 in revenge for the massacre of the English garrison. Earlier, the castle had been destroyed by the Scots themselves. The town burned for six days. David I in 1137 made the town to

14 Aberdeen: Castle Street. This should be a handsome street but it fails to delight. The large-scale massive Georgian façade diminishes its neighbours, and only the panache of the granite civic building opposite saves it from appearing inadequate. The white paint on the dormer windows makes them too prominent. The spaciousness of the street, its most distinguished feature, unfortunately allows for constant heavy traffic and the consequent untidy array of traffic signs.

the north a burgh of barony in favour of the bishop. St Machars Cathedral lay to the north.

After 1330 the citizens rebuilt their town first at Broadgate, a broad street joined to Gallowgate. The parish church of St Nicholas lay outside the burned town. It may not have had a site reserved within the burgh at first, for St Machars two miles away may have served the burgh in its early development up to the time when most plots were taken up. Nevertheless, the two churches may have been founded at dates close to one another.

By the end of the fourteenth century Castle Street became the major market(**14**).

Burgh rigs, meadows and muirs

An essential complement to the town plan was the provision of agricultural land for cultivation and grazing adjacent to the towns. The burgesses were to enjoy the right of receiving each year rigs for cultivation. These strips about 25 feet (7.62 metres) wide were produced by cutting draining channels as divisions and spreading the surplus top soil over the land on each side. To facilitate drainage, sloping sites were selected preferably with a south facing aspect. The locations of these may sometimes be detected on eighteenth-century or early nineteenth-century maps, and records in land ownership also preserve some of the boundaries. Examples are the area called the Roods at Inverkeithing, and the Burgh of Lauder in Berwickshire, where the allocation procedure among burgesses survived up to the end of the nineteenth century and was then described by Sir Henry Maine as 'the most perfect example of the primitive cultivating community extant in England [*sic*] or Germany'. The riverside haughs, then not drained, and the hilly areas were reserved for cattle and sheep grazing. The burgh muir would also provide timber for fuel, peat when available, and clay for the walls of buildings. The first essential requirement for a community, water, did not seem to have been a problem and probably then, as now, was recognised as one of Scotland's surplus commodities.

The first immigrants

With the plan prepared, the king needed people. They had to be men of substance with means to pay rent, acquire materials for house building, and obtain stock and equipment for their land. Some experience of purchasing and selling merchandise and arranging for its transport and sale in foreign markets would have been an advantage to the king. Finding men with experience of trade lay at the root of his urban policy because an advanced system of national foreign trade had not previously existed, and few opportunities to become involved in trade had been offered to local people. Many of the recruits, therefore, had to be brought from outwith the kingdom. It was to induce a flow of immigrants that the king granted every entrant to the planned towns the exclusive rights to buy and sell in the town and decreed that all producers from the countryside outside who wished to put their goods on offer could only do so through a merchant of a town which was ascribed to their area and chartered by the king or through his authority. When these merchants became burgesses, they enjoyed the king's peace, market monopoly and legally binding commercial dealing, but they were under obligation to pay rent and duties or tolls, and, as mentioned above, to share the duty of night-watch on the burgh's ports.

The native town dwellers

Exercising his strong Anglo-Norman connections, David turned to England, France and Flanders. Injection of immigrants from these countries by peaceful invasion brought to the new towns ambitious pioneers in quest of prosperity and wealth. Although this element must have constituted a sizeable majority of the burgesses, local people would also form part of the burgh populations. Some would continue to occupy houses which had existed before the new markets were planned, and others would rent land to pursue their crafts. These latter did not necessarily aspire to be merchants with the right to trade and to have a say in the administration of the town's affairs. These craft citizens may have been directed to the small short plots at the ends of the market-place where they could build their houses with probably a space or booth at the frontage to produce and display their work – as is still to be seen in small towns in the Far East. Among the first of the immigrants from Flanders was Baldwin, a lorimer by trade who had the support of David I and came to Perth (which also received weavers from Germany in the early thirteenth century). Some of the Flemings were mercenaries in the Scottish army which William the Lion modelled on the Flemish military science of the time. One indication of the number of immigrants is that David I addressed a charter concerning land in Garioch in French, English, Flemish and Scots. Mainard, one of the first burgesses in St Andrews, was Flemish and a burgess in Berwick. The master of the first Scottish mint at Roxburgh came from France at the request of David I.

The setting out of the new towns

The first towns called for planners who would have acquired the skill and techniques at a theoretical and practical level. They had to determine the size of the town, the area of its market and the dimensions of the plots. To transfer these needs on to a site in a workable way, a knowledge of soil characteristics and land drainage had to be acquired. Whatever had been first devised for the plan had to be measured and set out on site.

When Edward I initiated the new town of Berwick-on-Tweed, he ordered the men in twenty-four English towns to 'elect men from your wisest and ablest who know best how to devise, order and array a new town to the greatest profit to Ourselves and of Merchants'. The selected experts were presumably sent to Berwick. They included Sir Henry de Walys of London and Bordeaux whose experience had been gained in French town planning, and Thomas Alard, the planner of New Winchelsea, a town set out on gracious lines. It is likely that educated noblemen would have had a fair knowledge of town layout in the middle ages. At about the turn of the fourteenth century the Duke of Albany with a group of noblemen superintended the adjustment of Sandgate in Ayr to prevent the nuisance of blown sand into the area.

No evidence exists as to how these projects were realised on site. It could be assumed that prospective burgesses would arrive at intervals over a period, probably over many years. They would have to find shelter, initially either with local households or in an adjacent monastery, for there seems little doubt that most had the responsibility within one year of building their own homes, although perhaps with the assistance of craftsmen. Therefore the presence of established local residents would solve a number of practical problems in setting up new towns, and suggests a strong motive for the new burghs to be planned as significant town expansion schemes. Locals could prepare the sites by clearing scrub and removing large stones or infilling hollows in the market area. The king's agents would measure out the town or part of it at first, probably determining from a plan the principal boundary intersections on site by positioning march stones. The perimeter of the market, or part of it, would also then be fixed either by staking it out or by delineating it with a plough furrow. To improve drainage the plots may have been divided out on site by digging ditches and spreading the surplus soil, as on the cultivation rigs outwith the town. Evidence supporting this conjecture appears to have been obtained in recent archaeological investigation. The benefit of a dry site for building or for holding markets would have been appreciated then as much as to-day, for wet and freezing Scottish winters can turn attractive looking building ground of grassy loam and clay into an obstruction under foot resembling incipient primeval ooze.

As work progressed on the building, some of the successful first burgesses would have probably moved to more favourably located plots to build improved homes, leaving the old ones to new arrivals.

The influence of local topography

In modern times landscape is modified to suit buildings. In medieval times building was arranged to suit the natural landscape. This may not have been a conscious procedure. As has been demonstrated, medieval planners set out their towns to suit the topography, but they also very significantly paid attention to the direction that travellers had chosen to take in the years – if not centuries – before, when they went on foot across the terrain where the town was to be built. Medieval people, like their modern counterparts when they walk, selected the easiest way available, not necessarily the straightest. They reacted in a human way to the gradients and conditions under foot. It follows that when towns conform to the directions thus established, they too will reflect a human response to the natural conditions of the site. By conforming to these inherited influences, the planners conceived a fundamental principle. Properly sited towns, such as Coldstream, should drape the landscape as handsomely as a well tailored garment fits its wearer(**15**).

15 Coldstream. The perfection achieved in this town offers a lesson to planners: a good site above a river combines with roofs and planting which blend together, church towers which punctuate the skyline and an imposing column mounted at the bridge.

This principle of implanting towns into the countryside, 'burghculture', was clearly appreciated by observers of later generations when the towns still retained their unaltered shape. Montrose was one of the first royal towns to conform to this principle. Bishop Pococke 500 years later remarked on its most pleasant situation 'on an eminence that falls away in a beautiful manner'. The attractiveness of other burghs – such as Ayr(**16**), Dumfries, Dalkeith, St Andrews and many more – inspired artists in the eighteenth century and early nineteenth century to depict them in their surroundings, for at that time the towns had not yet begun to suffer from later ill-fitting additions as unbecoming as an off-the-peg duffle coat.

The building of the towns

It is still possible to picture these first new market towns and detect the influence of the genetic code with which they were imprinted in their early beginnings. They were low-density towns, about four houses, or just under twenty-five persons to the acre. The central market place fronting the houses was largely grassed over, and the rear of each plot or toft would be cultivated with vegetables, herbs, flowers and fruit trees. Immediately at the back of the houses lay the byres, poultry

16 Ayr: the Twa' Brigs, early nineteenth century. This scene shows a typical picturesque urban setting: town steeples, the river, the Auld Brig', New Adams Bridge, the toll, stagecoach, peep show and in front, the paviour's tools, including his rammer.

39

houses and pig sties. The houses were placed at, or close to, the front, positioned with their gables facing the market, and separated from their neighbours by a gate with posts, partly to prevent the escape of their animals on to the market, and partly the invasion into their ground of their neighbours' or market herds. The gate at the rear through a palisade would lead on to the cowgate to let out the cattle and other farm animals led by the herd down to the pastures by the loch or river, or up to summer grazing or the cultivated rigs after harvest and before planting – as at Lauder(**17**). Several of the plots would be amalgamated for the erection of the parish church and burial ground, and occasionally a large house or palace would occupy a combination of plots – as at Haddington(**VII**).

The market

The market was furnished with three essential items: the cross, the weigh house or tron, and the tolbooth. The cross was positioned at the centre of the market to establish where proclamations could be made, bargains could be struck and merchandise presented for inspection or sale(**18**). Its function had been thus defined from the twelfth century, and as time passed other activities became associated with it, such as festivities and punishment. To the burgh, the cross was therefore not merely what the striped pole was to the barber. Crosses were raised in even the small villages in Scotland. The earliest seem to have consisted of a wood shaft, plain with splayed corners or in the form of an octagon, set on three or

17 Lauder: Castle Wynd. A surviving medieval cowgate: on the left lies the burgh – urbanculture – and on the right, the fields – agriculture. The herdsmen led out the burgesses' herds in the morning and brought them back in the evening, each beast entering through its owner's back gate without any prompting from the herdsman.

18 Crail: Marketgate South. Part of a generously planned market-place, now embraced by well proportioned buildings completed by a good market cross and a typical robust Fife tolbooth.

more stone steps, finished with an ornamental top, and resembling the Christian cross only in name.

The weigh house may at first have consisted of an open balance large enough to weigh sacks of wool and so on. In later times some were placed, beneath a shelter. Their function, however, was eventually extended, and petty offenders were in some towns made to stand there, attached to the wooden frame by a nail pierced through their ear.

The trading taxes and customs were collected by the unpopular official agents, sometimes monks. Collection took place at booths, probably furnished with wooden covered counters. By a welcome process of civic metamorphosis these squalid little medieval VAT offices became the handsome Scottish tolbooths of later times(**19**).

The standard of building
There is understandable justification for dismissing these new towns as primitive and unattractive. Recent valuable archaeological work has confirmed the early use of timber construction either in forms of vertical planks or wattle techniques. But the evidence, perforce, derives mostly from the uncovering of rear building, and so the details of the main frontage buildings remain elusive. The few near contemporary records give the impression of impermanent jerry-building thrown up in a few days. A century and a half after these first towns had been built Froissart sneeringly observed that the Scots were not troubled when their houses were destroyed because they could rebuild them within three days with five or six poles and some branches. He coolly refrained from mentioning that when he and his plundering comrades had destroyed people's

19 Nairn. Unlike the High Streets of most Scottish burghs, this one is narrow and tends to be straight with parallel sides. Monotony has been prevented by the nineteenth-century architects who were given freedom to build in stone to designs of their choice. Standing above is the robust tower of the Town Chambers surmounted by a steepled lantern with clock. The inappropriate trivial contribution of the twentieth century shows why it is now sadly necessary to have planning control on building design in town centres.

homes, a temporary quick shelter for a man's family was his first consideration, and a victim would display a measure of nonchalance to deprive the marauders of some of their superior satisfaction.

Many of the burgesses who had settled in Scotland in the twelfth century or later had seen the best houses that countries of the medieval world around the North Sea could offer – better probably than those in England. These men could be expected to apply their knowledge to obtain accommodation equal to what they had enjoyed previously. They would not be content to exist in rough conditions any longer than necessity demanded in the early days of their pioneering. Local craftsmen had the opportunity to see the abbeys being erected because of the king's determination to bring the culture of the Church into Scotland, and some craftsmen would have been employed on the superior form of building that such work demanded. The burgesses' houses facing the market would be soundly constructed and timber-lined or infilled with framing and wattle and finished in clay. Roofs would be thatched, and some were tiled. Some may have had coloured walls, doors and so on. Most would be of two storeys. All would be neat and clean. Grouped round their curving market they would have presented a pleasing sight.

English clerks composing the record of the Scottish campaign of Edward I of England referred to the Scottish examples of town building such as Forfar, Montrose(**20**) and Elgin (**21**) as fine towns, and to Aberdeen and St Andrews as good towns. Accustomed to the less disciplined, more relaxed plans of English towns, they would have been understandably impressed by the order and clarity of the Scottish towns.

The influence of the monasteries in the twelfth and thirteenth centuries

The abbeys and monasteries did not only strengthen the intellectual and religious development of the country. They extended the limitations of local agriculture, husbandry and mineral exploitation. Coal mining was started in East Lothian. Salt pans were made by the abbeys in the Borders, Fife and the Lothians, and sheep were introduced, all in the thirteenth century. Dundrennen Abbey produced surplus grain for export to England. The Black Friars, Dominicans, were strongly represented before the end of the thirteenth century. Alexander II made them the gift of the Royal Gardens at Perth overlooking the Tay and the North Insch. The most active in gardening later

20 Montrose. Dating from 1124-53, this is one of the finest planned burghs in the country. It is wide, spacious and perfectly sited on a rising ridge. The curving sides and the closures at the ends and near the centre demonstrate the value of a soundly arranged ground plan, one which has been evident for centuries and admired by previous generations.

21 Elgin: High Street. Elgin is one of the most graceful towns in Scotland and a tribute to medieval planning (1136–53). The curve of the plan closes off the street at the foot, and the statue, column, fountain and trees enhance the superior design of the street. The flat-roofed recent buildings with their pin-eyed windows look unfinished and comatose.

in the following century were the Carthusians at Perth and the Vallis Caulium monks at Beauly. The Tyronensian House also maintained well kept gardens and orchards, particularly at Kilwinning, Lindores and Lesmahagow. To Arbroath went the responsibility for first cultivating cabbages in Scotland.

The Cistercian order cultivated trees at Balmerino which were admired all over Fife, and specimens from their gardens, such as chestnut, elm and walnut trees, survived for centuries after the Middle Ages. The Abbey of the Cistercians at Cupar had a garden for growing herbs and flowers and a well stocked orchard. These developments were achieved by the various orders importing new varieties from their mother churches in France and England. Seeds and young plants propagated from the imports were sold to the royal gardens and probably later were further distributed to gardens in the burghs. The monasteries set a high example of gardening for the medieval burgesses, and from them the burgesses would have acquired the techniques needed to grow orchards and vegetables to add to the delights of the local herbs and flowers such as wallflowers, musk, mallow and sweet violet.

The influence of the monasteries was fairly widespread because by the end of the thirteenth century all the monastic houses were nearly complete, except that Sweetheart Abbey had been founded late (1273) and the Carthusians had not yet arrived in Scotland. Over a score of friaries were established. The presence of shrines at monasteries brought influence to bear on the siting and development of some of the burghs, notably St Andrews, Glasgow, Canongate, Brechin, Dunfermline and Peebles. At a lesser level, monasteries attracted outside their precincts craftsmen such as millers, waulkers and brewers, for the monks enjoyed their beer.

3 Towns in the Reigns of Malcolm IV (1153-65) and William the Lion (1165-1214), and the Golden Age of Alexander II (1214-49) and Alexander III (1249-86)

The strife which was cruelly to blight Scottish life and towns over several centuries still lay a long way ahead. Malcolm IV and William the Lion followed David I and kept the momentum of town making at the forefront of national policy. Thus by 1214 a further fourteen royal burghs had been planned and chartered, and the nobles had received authority to add a further eight. It is also likely that some burghs established before this period – such as Perth, Edinburgh and probably St Andrews, Linlithgow and Stirling – had began to expand.

Lanark

The typical form of market-place continued to be followed in royal burgh planning, as at Ayr, Dumfries, Inverkeithing and Arbroath. The evolution of Lanark especially reveals the process of change and expansion that was being pursued (**IX**). Before the royal burgh was planned Lanark developed along the approach to Lanark Castle situated on Castle Hill. The site of the

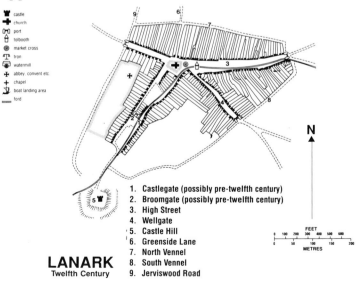

legend:
- ♛ castle
- ✠ church
- ⬗ port
- ⌷ tolbooth
- ◉ market cross
- ⬍ tron
- ⬖ watermill
- ✚ abbey, convent etc.
- ✝ chapel
- ⬎ boat landing area
- ▬▬▬ ford

N

LANARK
Twelfth Century

1. Castlegate (possibly pre-twelfth century)
2. Broomgate (possibly pre-twelfth century)
3. High Street
4. Wellgate
5. Castle Hill
6. Greenside Lane
7. North Vennel
8. South Vennel
9. Jerviswood Road

FEET
0 100 200 300 400 500 600
0 50 100 150 200
METRES

Map IX Lanark, twelfth century. The Castle, Broomgate and Castlegate preceded the planned town of the twelfth century at High Street. Wellgate also probably preceded High Street.

castle on its bluff lay to the south of the route that followed in a south-easterly direction by what is now Greenside Lane, Wellgate, Wellgate Head, the old parish church of St Kentigern and on to the Hyndford Road. The approach to the castle from this route would have been by way of Castlegate. The first houses to be built would have been clustered round the foot of Castlegate, and occupied by retainers and servants of the castle in a similar way to the early occupation of Castle Hill at Edinburgh Castle. From this beginning the town first grew round a small market area formed by modern Broomgate – Castlegate up to about the point where No. 73 Castlegate is situated. This early market-place was then extended further north up Castlegate with houses built on deeper plots on the east side. The depths of the plots on the west side may have been later curtailed in the fourteenth century to accommodate the Franciscan friary.

The market-place which this first town provided apparently was eventually not considered adequate. Although the town was not well placed geographically for foreign trade, it had an expansive landward area which offered good opportunities for regional trading in wool, hides and dairy produce, resembling in this respect Roxburgh and Haddington. With the enterprise and energy typical of Scotland at the time, a new market-place was planned. The site selected lay to the north-east of the town on the line of the burn which turned and ran through Castlegate. This burn may have been an artificial watercourse built at an earlier time to serve the domestic needs of the town and provide a ditch to the castle. The market, now High Street, was laid out on more spacious lines and was probably 15–20 feet (4.5–6 metres) wider than its present width of 50–100 feet (15.2–3.04 metres), although otherwise it still survives. The North and South Vennels provided the cowgates. The long rigs on the south side of the market had to be set at an acute angle to the frontage because of their junction with Wellgate. Here the planners failed. Wellgate on the line of the old route was left to squeeze out awkwardly between the heads of the old market-place and High Street. It was a makeshift solution then and has remained so ever since. Probably it was hoped that the alternative to the original route by way of High Street to the junction of Ladyacre Road and the Hyndford Road would supersede the older route which might then have gone into disuse. However, the old route was more direct and led to an important well in the centre of the road, and to the south of the town, and these advantages were not to be abandoned. When Bloomgate was made and occupied, and the West Port built at its end by the entrance to the North Vennel, the access from the north and west changed from Greenside Lane on the old route to a new route on the line of Jarviswood Road to arrive at the port or gate giving entry to the burgh.

Despite its defect this medieval plan of Lanark has survived. Building up was allowed in the centre of the first market-place as it fell into disuse. In the late twelfth century the space at the junction of the market-place and High Street was seen to be the perfect site for St Nicholas Church. A new coaching road was driven through the north-west in the eighteenth century into Bloomgate, but the fine modern town centre confirms the benefit of fine medieval planning. Mercifully a Town Council of recent years knew this and unhesitantly rebuffed a comprehensive but inept scheme of modernisation.

Ayr

When Ayr was granted its charter it probably had made a brave start by building a small simply planned market-place on Sandgate which was on the route from the south to the ford crossing the River Ayr. The castle stood on the west by the river on its way to the Firth of Clyde. It was likely that the town then had a cross and a tolbooth. But like other medieval towns, Ayr expanded to an orderly planned scheme placing its larger more modern High Street back at an angle to the earlier Sandgate on a north-south axis, unusual in the south of Scotland. This was done by employing a right-angled link at the foot of the two streets. In its shape and connecting route with Sandgate, the newer plan laid down the ground work for the burgh's evolution.

Dumfries

Dumfries, the first town in the south-west of the country to receive its Royal Charter (*c.* 1186), probably began at a much earlier date (**X**). A ford across the Nith towards Nith Place could have led to the Annan and Lochmaben routes possibly in the earliest period of the town – in or before the eleventh century. The more direct way on the line of Shakespeare Street may have been too marshy then so that the loop on the English Street direction would have been more practicable, especially during winter. The drier ridge of the present High Street would then have been followed towards the Motte, at which point the route would have turned approximately north along the way now constituting Townhead Street.

Difficulty arises in explaining the position and alignment of the Old Bridge up stream from the ford. It seems possible that it was preceded by a wooden bridge. Had its erection been achieved before the middle of the thirteenth century the direction could be explained on the reasonable assumption that it would have been directly joined to the Townhead Street route towards which the present bridge points. Thereafter on the introduction of the Greyfriars Convent, in 1260, Friars' Vennel

Map X Dumfries, twelfth–thirteenth century. The royal burgh was soundly planned on a ridge and furnished with a wide market which still gives the town great dignity. A north–south orientation is unusual in southern Scotland.

castle
church
port
tolbooth
market cross
tron
watermill
abbey convent etc
chapel
boat landing area
ford

1. High Street
2. Nith Place
3. Shakespeare Street
4. English Street
5. Townhead Street
6. Friars Vennel
7. Loreburn Street

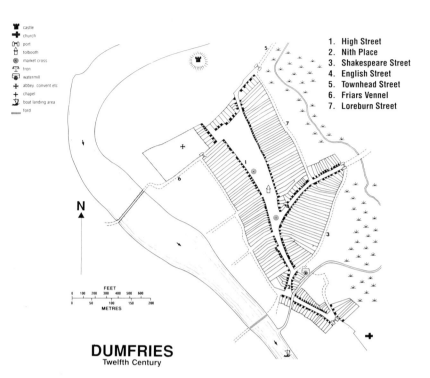

N

FEET
0 100 200 300 400 500 600
0   50   100   150   200
METRES

DUMFRIES
Twelfth Century

22 Dumfries: High Street, 1843. The town setting radiates energy. From its conception in 1186 it seems to have been destined to retain its splendid urban character.

was substituted to the south-east of the more direct line to make way for the Convent Garden. It requires this analysis or some other explanation to account for the inconvenient entry (which prevailed well into the nineteenth century) via Loreburn Street into High Street from the important road from the north–east. Church Street was not formed until near the middle of the nineteenth century.

The first settlement along St Michael Street saw the beginning of the town which was associated with the twelfth-century St Michael's Church and was located at the limit of the navigable river with its beach to land boats and its adjacent ford. The distance separating this early town from the Motte to the north-west need not preclude this supposition.

The new market-place was later set off along the slight ridge with the valley of the Nith on its west side and Loreburn, which in the twelfth century flowed on the east of the cowgate, now Loreburn Street. The new market thus laid out, without its central intrusions, followed in shape and plan the familiar form of the royal burghs of that time: the castle stood at the head of the market, but was set back from the buildings for defence purposes. Its expanse, measuring nearly 1,150 feet (350 metres) in length and at its greatest width 250 feet (76.2 metres), thus provided an area of about 4½ acres (1.82 hectares), showing that Dumfries was expected to become the centre of trade in the south-west (**22**).

Arbroath

Arbroath may have existed in a simple form when the abbey was founded between 1187 and 1195. A group of fishermen's houses along the shore at a point near Seagate where boats could be safely beached would have marked the terminal of a route leading north by ferry mainly to Montrose and Aberdeen(**XI**). The medieval market-place or High Street probably followed this route, but it was diverted round the abbey precinct before the end of the twelfth century – accounting for the sudden change of direction at Kirk Square. The Marketgate, like the medieval supplementary markets of other towns (such as Edinburgh, St Andrews, Perth and Peebles) was planned later. The essential character of the plan was not impaired by the abbey siting on higher ground to the north of High Street because that relationship resulted in what must have been an impressive prospect towards the north reached from round the curving High Street to the south and framed by the houses on either side.

Inverkeithing

The medieval market-place at Inverkeithing is almost rectangular, like those in some of the other early towns in Fife.

Map XI Arbroath, twelfth century. Like St Andrews, Arbroath was a twelfth-century bishop's burgh dominated by an important abbey. Like Perth, it later expanded by planning the Market Gate.

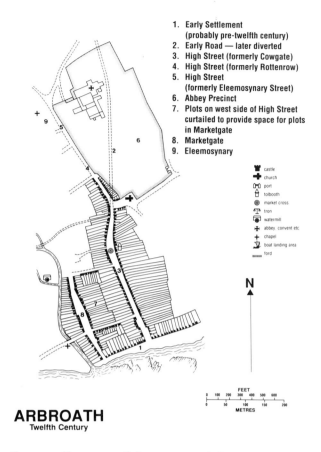

1. Early Settlement (probably pre-twelfth century)
2. Early Road — later diverted
3. High Street (formerly Cowgate)
4. High Street (formerly Rottenrow)
5. High Street (formerly Eleemosynary Street)
6. Abbey Precinct
7. Plots on west side of High Street curtailed to provide space for plots in Marketgate
8. Marketgate
9. Eleemosynary

castle
church
port
tolbooth
market cross
tron
watermill
abbey, convent etc
chapel
boat landing area
ford

N

FEET
0 100 200 300 400 500 600
0   50   100   150   200
METRES

ARBROATH
Twelfth Century

23 Inverkeithing. Post-war housing on the fringe of the historic centre shows how the layout of buildings can be planned to enliven local character.

Its small area of just over 1.8 acres (0.61 hectares), although probably planned to a wider and longer dimension, suggests trade was relatively slight, and the town's acknowledged importance in the twelfth century was directed more towards its harbour and shipping facilities. Its siting along the contours on cross-falling ground likely derived from an existing near northward orientated route and a junction of a route to the east. The burgh roods lay on the west and south-west on ground with a nearly southerly aspect to obtain the best conditions for cultivation and growth. Port Street connected the top of the market by the parish church at High Street down to the bay where there may have been an earlier settlement.

The building up of the two island sites, because of the restricted area available for the market, may not have occurred until after medieval times. The composition of the plan focussing on the parish church was excellent, but overbuilding round the church does not now reveal it. Inverkeithing, however, is another example of a town satisfyingly located in its surroundings, and it is still possible to appreciate how well medieval planners related burghculture to agriculture, and how sympathetic planning can maintain character(**23**).

Glasgow

This period also saw the rise of Glasgow and Dundee. Glasgow seems to have put much of its energies into cathedral building. The old route from the ford over the Clyde led up to the former shrine and the cathedral, following an 'S' bend near the precincts to ease the gradient. A second route traversed along the upper, drier north bank of the Clyde on the line of the medieval Trongate and Gallowgate. Where these naturally formed routes crossed, the burgh of Glasgow was founded in the twelfth century.

It would have extended up High Street from the cross about 300 feet (91.4 metres), west along Trongate for about the same length, and east along Gallowgate to the west of the Molendinar Burn at a ford or bridge. Market Street would have extended down Saltmarket Street to the point where Bridgegate Street was later built. At the end of the following century expansion along Bridgegate Street would have commenced, and building up High Street must have nearly reached a length equal to Saltmarket Street to stop at the point where the Blackfriars' monastery was established in the middle of the thirteenth century. Houses of people who served the cathedral would have been built independently close by, leaving a gap of open country between the commercial and cathedral centres. The result of these events does not seem to reveal the hand of a master planner, and until the nineteenth century, town making seldom ever counted among the very considerable accomplishments of the city.

Dundee

Dundee, promoted locally with royal assent, was planned on generous lines. A small settlement to the east of the castle on Seagate may have already been established along with Cowgate to the north. It was reputed to have possessed in early times a mercat cross and tolbooth east of Horse Wynd. The new burgh was planned in the twelfth century to the west of the castle with a tapering market place and High Street which probably extended along to the first St Mary's Church founded in 1189(**XII**). It contained a cross and tron. The plots reached back on the north to 400 feet (122 metres) and south down a shorter distance to the shore as it existed at that time (West Shore). Overgate and Nethergate led through the ports into the corners of the market-place on each side of the church. At a later period the route to the north-east and north was formed by Murraygate and Wellgate.

Agriculture was as usual practiced on the south-facing slopes of the roods east and west of Hilltown, with the grazing meadow and stream north of High Street entered by Meadow Entry and other passages off Wellgate convenient to Cowgate. The

Map XII Dundee, twelfth–thirteenth century. The lively plan of the twelfth century remained almost intact up to the twentieth century and then was ignored and largely destroyed.

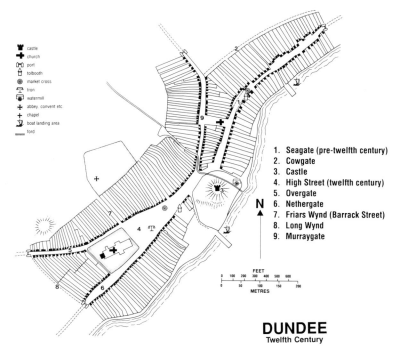

castle
church
port
tolbooth
market cross
tron
watermill
abbey, convent etc
chapel
boat landing area
ford

1. Seagate (pre-twelfth century)
2. Cowgate
3. Castle
4. High Street (twelfth century)
5. Overgate
6. Nethergate
7. Friars Wynd (Barrack Street)
8. Long Wynd
9. Murraygate

N

FEET
0 100 200 300 400 500 600
0   50   100   150   200
METRES

DUNDEE
Twelfth Century

monastery also occupied a site immediately north of the town wall. Apart from some infilling of High Street in front of St Mary's Church and some building-up of closes, Dundee retained its splendid form for more than 600 years(**24, 25**). The insecurity of towns nowadays is demonstrated by recent events, where Bonnie Dundee, like the Fairy Prince, is in danger of being transformed by the modern city witch-doctors into a urban toad.

Crail

As has been illustrated, the plans of the period generally conformed to the first medieval pattern. They followed the preconditioned 'influence lines', were effectively controlled on site and employed the same techniques in any extension. Crail may have grown in three phases(**XIII**). The small village by the harbourage lay close within the protection of the castle. It would have been reached by paths from the coastal route above which likely followed along the line of Westgate, High Street and Marketgate. This first market would seem to have spread towards the east from the castle to about Tolbooth Street, formed in the shape of a triangle without the much later central intrusions. The second phase, possibly of the twelfth century, appeared to have repeated the shape of the first market by widening the main route on the north side up to West Green, and this became High Street, again without the later central encroachment dug into the cross slope. The spacious Marketgate

24 Dundee: Tendall's Wynd. From medieval times merchants, goods and invading armies travelled up and down this ancient route between the harbour, market and castle. The narrow width made it easily defensible in time of attack and gave shelter from the wind.

followed along with the parish church founded on its eastern extremity. This last market covered nearly 2 acres (0.81 hectares), measuring 650 feet by 130 feet (198 × 39.6 metres). Despite the cross-falls the roads and wynds connecting the lower to the upper towns have acceptable gradients of about 1 in 19.5 on the east, 1 in 23 at the centre, and the original route, 1 in 18.8. This final plan became the chief market-place with its

25 Dundee: Fish Street. Once the address of persons of quality, Fish Street declined and largely disappeared in the late nineteenth century. It had managed to retain the rhythm of its medieval frontages when these tall houses were erected with varied design approaches – ogee gables, Venetian windows, ground floor piazza, gable dormers and the notable tower (**31**).

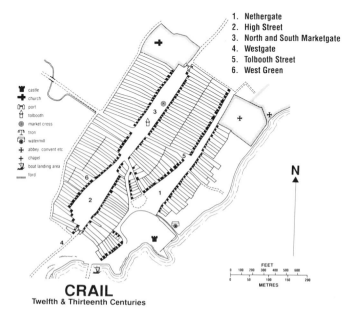

1. Nethergate
2. High Street
3. North and South Marketgate
4. Westgate
5. Tolbooth Street
6. West Green

castle
church
port
tolbooth
market cross
tron
watermill
abbey. convent etc
chapel
boat landing area
ford

N

FEET
0 100 200 300 400 500 600
0   50   100   150   200
METRES

CRAIL
Twelfth & Thirteenth Centuries

Map XIII Crail, twelfth–thirteenth century. A twelfth-century plan that was skilfully extended in the thirteenth century to achieve a most imaginative town.

tolbooth and cross(**18**). The whole creation endorses the skill of Scottish medieval planning. A clear plan is conceived in its main elements and comfortably eased and moulded on to the site after the natural contour and the humanly produced tracks have been observed and understood.

Urban conditions in the thirteenth century

Scottish towns thrived in the thirteenth century. The weather favoured farming. Foreign trade expanded. Culture spread with the completion through the century of the monastic establishments, and the country had a sufficiency of churches and schools for Latin to be taught. The merchant guilds were reorganised early in the century, but craftsmen remained in an inferior position without organisation. The burghs became more ambitious in the scope of their trading. Ships arrived at Leith, Perth, Berwick and other ports with cargoes from the Red Sea, the Mediterranean and the East Indies. King's Lynn sent corn, peas, beans, salt, barley and wine. Salted herring were brought in from Norway and Yarmouth. The abbeys also traded abroad in England and Ireland. The standard of living to be enjoyed in Scotland in these early times by the landowners, merchants and successful craftsmen demanded importation of delicacies like ginger, almonds and rice, and flavourings such as pepper, garlic and onions – desirable for making the winter's salted meat more palatable. The continent provided culinary articles, locks for doors, safes in the form of iron-bound chests to safeguard money and valuables, and building materials. Scotland supplied its own meat, fruit and food and exported hides, leather, wool and salmon, oak, deer hide and lambskin.

The country's greatest gift during this period, however, was comparative peace. Some uprisings in the north and west of the country had to be put down, and Alexander III drove the Norsemen out of the Hebrides. To Haddington in 1216 went the dubious distinction of being the first victim of that sport of English kings and their nobility, the burning of Scottish towns. The surrounding countryside including Dunbar was of course not spared.

Scotland was also probably visited by the pestilence that afflicted England in the second half of the century and into the fourteenth century. The outbreaks may have been mild because Scotland's climate seems somehow to offer protection in such matters – just as in freedom from death-watch beetle and the less devastating effect of Dutch Elm disease.

The prosperity resulted in the development of the foreign trade of the existing burghs and in the granting of royal charters to six new burghs. Two notable new royal burghs were Dumbarton (1222) and Wigtown (1292), which still strictly conformed to the plan of the twelfth century(**XIV**). Kelso also

Map XIV Wigtown, late thirteenth century. Although planned much later than other royal burghs, Wigtown retained the usual medieval form.

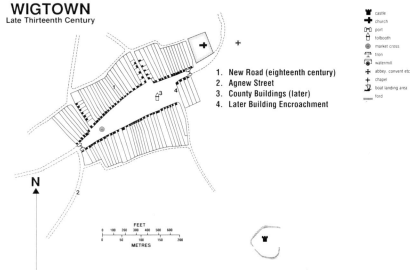

WIGTOWN
Late Thirteenth Century

1. New Road (eighteenth century)
2. Agnew Street
3. County Buildings (later)
4. Later Building Encroachment

castle
church
port
tolbooth
market cross
tron
watermill
abbey, convent etc
chapel
boat landing area
ford

N

FEET
0 100 200 300 400 500 600
0 50 100 150 200
METRES

became a bishop's burgh, and some of the burghs of barony were created. The number of charters granted, however, does not reveal the true extent to which the number of towns grew. Many were founded on local trade before they eventually became officially recognised. Such late-comers to chartered status included Musselburgh, Dunbar(**26**), Dalkeith, Lochmaben, Cupar(**27**), Kirkcudbright, Selkirk(**6**), Lauder, Rothesay, North Berwick, Tain, Falkland(**28**) and Paisley.

The urban evolution of the country during the 'Golden Age of Scottish History' grew out of the earlier planned towns. These

26 Dunbar. The High Street of this well preserved town is undergoing the natural process of evolution. There are good examples of Georgian and Victorian frontages still conforming to the medieval widths of 24 to 26 feet (7.3 to 8 metres). Properly composed individual buildings such as the Town House and the George Hotel fit well where the street widens to 85 feet (26 metres), and no pre-packaged fast-built supermarket architecture has slipped through the planning net.

27 Cupar: Crossgate. This medieval plan has survived even though two severe conflagrations destroyed most of its seventeenth-century buildings. From the late eighteenth century many new simple classical buildings were followed by richer stone-built designs, as the photograph illustrates. This inspired a local minister to remark in both flattery and disapproval that the town bore the appearance of a clean and comfortable English town.

had been organised for trade and development on a regional and national scale. From the years of the initial uncomplicated form they began to acquire a more complete organisation. In several of the powerful burghs the merchants had formed themselves into guilds which began to take responsibility for selecting the council. The power which they enjoyed as burgesses from the initial royal privilege of monopoly over trade reached over into the direction of the courts in their respective burghs. The original purpose of the burghs had become both more extensive and wider in scope. In the natural process of urban evolution physical changes would inevitably follow.

Milling

The production of grain called for more intensive milling. The authorities turned to water power. Most towns where a suitable river lay nearby cut leads and in a few instances made dams. To drive the water wheel obviously entailed a large undertaking requiring skill in civil engineering. For this reason many mills belonged to the king. Burghs at the centre of grain production territory had several mills before the end of the thirteenth century; Haddington, for example, had three mills, one of which belonged to the adjacent monastery. Lanark, although it had increasing demands, did not have a burgh mill because the town was bound to use the mill on the River Mouse which was privately owned. Grain mills had also been built at Annan, Auchtermuchty, Kinghorn, Lauder, Linlithgow, Montrose, Selkirk, Perth, Peebles, St Andrews, Stirling, Dumfries, Inverness and many more towns. Rivers dictated their siting, and the roads to the mills and the mill leads came to influence the planning of towns and their future extensions. The increase in the wool trade was supported in the late thirteenth century by introducing water power to drive the machinery in waulk fulling mills, where cloth was soaked and beaten to shrink it and improve its quality.

Changes in houses

The physical change that would have been most striking over the century related to the houses. It seems that as time passed houses assumed a more urban appearance and were altered or rebuilt with the frequency which was possible when timber construction was employed. The first houses may have been more rural in character – low, narrow buildings with gable ends facing the market-place. By the start of the thirteenth century, examples of longer façades facing the frontage had begun to appear. Also, two-storey buildings containing stores on the

28 Falkland. This rich centre in a very small burgh informally gathers together the ancient royal palace, the steeple, an elaborate market cross and some old cottages of Scottish character.

ground floor and a house on the upper floor seemed to have become preferred by burgesses. Greater affluence would allow burgesses to finish the exteriors with more attention to style in the details of doors and windows.

Life in the towns in the thirteenth century
Mentions in contemporary records of booths in Inverness and Perth and of shops in surrounding villages show that some burghs were already about to undergo a change from an agricultural-trading community towards a more commercially orientated society. Although thatched roofs may have predominated, some pantiled roofs could have been seen in the more prosperous burghs like Berwick or Perth, and stone may have been used in the lower floors. But although examples of vaulted ground floors became common towards the end of the fifteenth century(**29**), they may not yet have been used in the burghs by the end of the thirteenth century. Stone building in the monasteries and churches would have enriched the architectural quality of the towns. Timber building, however, was still the main walling material even in the royal castles.

Many burghs seemed to appear compact because all the plots had been taken up and towns were being enlarged. This process was most strikingly observed in dominant burghs – Edinburgh, Perth, Stirling, Linlithgow, St Andrews and Berwick. Edinburgh's population could have increased by about 400 in the thirteenth century giving a total of nearly 2,000 persons, well above the average of about 800.

However, the burghs would have still maintained their agricultural bases with the farm animals kept at night and in winter at the rear of each plot. The craftsmen would work at the front or rear of the house, and it is thought that some craftsmen may have been subordinated to a richer merchant who would make room for them in buildings of simple construction on ground at the rear of their own houses. Work would begin with the early morning milking. The town herdsman would drive the cattle collected along the cowgates to the pastures. Bakers and brewsters made the bread and ale. The calls of the farm animals would mingle with the noises of the craftsmen such as smiths, shoemakers and tanners, of children playing, scholars singing in the choir school – for chapels were used by schoolmasters from the thirteenth or fourteenth centuries.

The burgh minstrel on occasions would play music on his instrument – often the bagpipes, for these were known in many of the medieval towns in Europe. He also lent colour to the scene, for in the fifteenth century he belonged to the exclusive category of townspeople who were exempted from the austerity laws banning coloured clothes below the knees or the wearing of silk. It may have been during the thirteenth century that songs

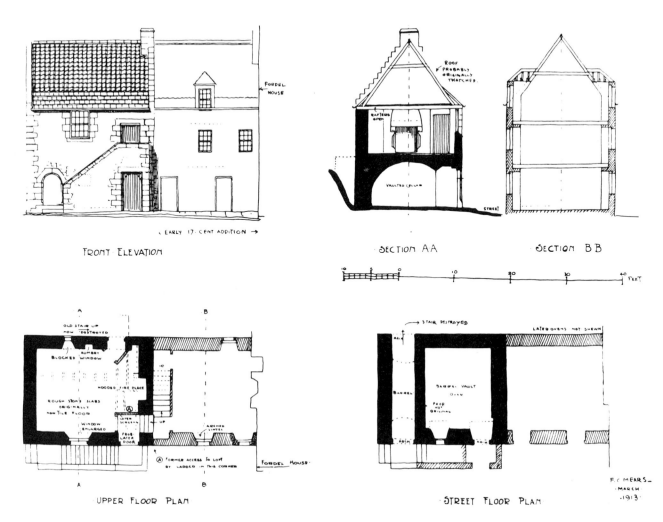

FRONT ELEVATION   SECTION AA   SECTION BB

UPPER FLOOR PLAN   STREET FLOOR PLAN

F.C.MEARS.
MARCH
1913

29 Inverkeithing: late fifteenth-century burgess's house. A drawing of an early stone-built burgess's house which was cleared about 1920 to make way for the town's war memorial.

were composed by the town minstrel and adopted by the burghs as their community song for festive and other events – as at Dumbarton, Linlithgow or Berwick.

These flourishing medieval burghs with their simple sanitation, cess pits, stables, byres and pig styes, tan yards and brew houses may suggest an odoriferous experience somewhat richer than what a modern refined sense of smell would be expected to tolerate. Conditions in these open towns would have been tempered by the sweeter surrounding country air. Edinburgh or Stirling, rising high above their surroundings, could never have been short of fresh air, and if the people of Edinburgh in the thirteenth century breathed the air of the farm and brewery, those in the twentieth century inhale the fumes of diesel oil, petrol, and still the brewery.

The first burghs may not have been colourless. Clothes were not all a drab 'hodden grey', for some burghs had tincters – dyers who would dye material in colours such as purple, saffron, blue, red and green. The interiors of churches and abbeys employed colour in decoration and some colourful flags, bunting and banners would be on show on the few fair days each year, or on royal occasions. The churches enjoyed fine singing, for boys at church song schools were taught music and Latin for the church services.

Market days were probably not noisy because buyers and sellers would bargain in tones not to be overheard – as Defoe found at the Leeds cloth market in the early eighteenth century. But when market hours were over, signalled by an announcement, or in Berwick by a bell, youths and young men may have cleared away the stalls and played football.

There is nothing to suggest that thirteenth-century urban life in Scotland was not socially and economically rewarding. The success of the towns and their competitiveness in foreign markets may have brought satisfaction to Scots, but it engendered covetousness in their neighbours.

4 The Wars of Independence in the Fourteenth to Sixteenth Centuries and the Urban Struggle for Survival

The first invasion

The end of the thirteenth century brought catastrophe. Edward I had revealed his grasping ambition towards Scotland. The Scottish king had died and now, quoth Edward, the successor must acknowledge our superiority over Scotland. This was the Edward whom Thomas Gray addressed in 'The Bard': 'Ruin seize thee, ruthless King! Confusion on thy banners wait!' These lines were written, of course, four hundred years after the events depicted.

Edward's intentions presented an impossible situation to the Scots because everyone knows that no power on earth can disillusion an Englishman once he feels a sense of his inborn superiority. An ill prepared force of Scots made an unsuccessful assault on Carlisle and immediately Edward with an army of highly trained cavalry and infantry crossed the Tweed. The loyal Berwick burgesses shut the gates of the ports on him, but the wooden palisades were breached by the invaders and the citizens of Berwick were unmercifully put to the sword and the town sacked. The accounts of the time claimed 7,000 perished, but exaggeration – an almost universal failing of military historians – must have been employed, for Berwick's population, even if swollen by refugees, was very much less than that number. The king displayed his gallantry by being first to reach the wall on his charger Bayard. His brave example and that of the Scottish kings were not in later years to be followed by the English nobles in their battles with Scotland, for they were usually to be found, like the Duke of Plaza-Toro, leading from behind.

Edward's Scottish campaign swept through the country, taking every town and castle of note and finishing back at the English border in the course of twenty-one weeks in the summer of 1296. By any standard, it was a *blitzkrieg* of momentous proportions. The army was said to have consisted of 30,000 infantry and 4,000 cavalry, again likely an exaggeration, but to march through Scotland from Coldstream to Elgin and back to Castleton taking every castle and town on the way, was a feat of military prowess seldom excelled.

These events did not at this stage seriously affect the burghs and their castles. The latter had been taken because Edward produced his secret weapon, siege machinery of a strength and effectiveness not known in Scotland. The Scots had relied on their castles in a 'Maginot Line' frame of mind and paid the inevitable penalty. Edward did not need to use his war engines after their power had been demonstrated at Edinburgh Castle, and his troops were not called upon to destroy towns or castles which fell without much if any resistance. Edward's intention was to take Scotland intact and exploit it for his own profit. It would not serve his purpose to destroy the burghs.

The English army had conquered Scotland but it could not succeed in pacifying its people. The Pope some years later reminded Edward that Scotland pertained to the Church and not to his ancestors. Edward exploded when told of this affront to his royal will. He replied to the Pope, in unctuous terms, that his claims over Scotland went back to the time of Eli and Samuel the prophet, hoping to impress with this biblical connection. The Scots, warming to the task, wrote in their turn that Scotland was descended from Scota, old Pharaoh's daughter, and had nothing to do with Edward. They pointed out that Edward had got his lineage mixed up, for he was directly descended from William the Bastard, and his accomplices. His Holiness, doubtless having already assessed his man, would have granted that this piece of intelligence explained much. After the fighting and retaking of castles by the Scots, Edward set out for Carlisle to lead the hosts he had summoned to descend upon Scotland once again. He was a man of tough fibre for, mortally ill, he had himself borne on a litter, but by merciful providence it transpired that the Hammer of the Scots had dealt his final blow, and he died before he could cross the border. It was rumoured that an English knight saw in a vision old Edward, on his way to the everlasting bonfire, being tormented by the devils of Hell. The vision was not complete, for it did not reveal whether the demons managed to disengage from the encounter unscathed.

The war continued. Truces were shattered by outbreaks of violence and fighting. The burghs at first suffered from the interruption of their foreign trade, the heavy costs of rebuilding their towns, and the action of pirates even during periods of solemn truce. The English kings seldom intervened in these violations, preserving an air of innocence when confronted with protests.

On one occasion pirates seized a ship off Yorkshire and put to death the whole ship's complement, including women and pilgrims bound for Compostello. These were times of ruthlessness. When the English kings captured leaders of the Scottish Resistance movement they had them marched to London and brought before a court, the high sounding name of which did not conceal its kangaroo character. They heard the evidence against the prisoner, took no evidence in defence, and refused the right of reply. They then dutifully gave their verdict as required by the king. The victim was dragged through the streets at the tail of a horse to the scaffold. He was hanged, cut down while still alive, and his vitals torn out and burned. The corpse was then hacked into manageable portions which were despatched to various towns and put on public display.

The castles

The chronicler of Edward I conveniently listed the important castles, generally on the east of the country, in the late thirteenth century. Castle Sween, of early design, was probably of stone not usual at that time, for nearly all castles were timber structures. Castles were mentioned at Aberdeen – 'a fair castle', Auchterarder, Balledgarno – 'the Red Castle', Dundee, Elgin – 'a good castle', Forfar, Fyvie, Inverness, Kildrummy, Montrose and St Andrews. Edinburgh and Stirling possessed their great fortresses from the twelfth century, and Bothwell was built of stone perhaps even earlier than Castle Sween. The castles at Perth and Crail probably belonged to the twelfth century and Auldearn and Invercullen to the thirteenth century. In the early fourteenth century, England held the castles of Berwick, Dirleton, Dundee, Edinburgh, Jedburgh, Linlithgow, Livingston, Luffness, Roxburgh and Selkirk. Other castles of fourteenth-century origin include Drum in Aberdeenshire, Glamis, Rothesay, Caerlaverock (a shell-form of castle unique in Scotland, based on the Welsh design favoured by Edward I, although probably built by Scots), Crichton and Tantallon – both in East Lothian – the latter having a site both romantic and militarily formidable. The plainness of Lochleven Castle is outweighed by its stirring association two hundred years later with Mary, Queen of Scots. Threave in Kirkcudbrightshire, an impressive square tower, stands on its island site in the River Dee. Craigmillar Castle, situated on an eminence close to Edinburgh, stood in strength until it was sacked in the sixteenth century by Hertford after he had accepted its surrender on the promise that he would not sack it – a typical Hertford tactic. When covetous eyes are cast on their companies, castles or country, Scots should beware of visitors pledging promises or bearing gifts. The ruins of Castle Duffus in Morayshire, of fourteenth-century date, represent a good example of 'motte-and-bailey' style. Hermitage, with its well preserved external remains in Roxburgh, occupies an ancient fortified site, but belongs to the fourteenth century.

The designs of these castles, many built at isolated points of vantage, had a twofold bearing on the burghs. The ultimate exclusive use of stone, preferably in broached ashlar, established a technique of masonry which became the adopted method of building in the first stone buildings in the towns, for instance, in Pittenweem(**30**). Also, the form of building a tall tower with

30 Pittenweem: High Street. The frontages follow a tremulous line towards the church, becoming lower in height to stop below the handsome tower. The gnarled late sixteenth-century house remains like a sentinel and makes a telling contribution to the composition.

vaulted ground floor and several timber upper floors influenced the planning of the first stone mansion houses in the burghs. Two examples are the New Wark in Dumfries, a tower with vaulted ground floor built in the fourteenth-century market-place and demolished in the middle of the eighteenth century, and the old tower in Fish Street in Dundee(**31**).

The burning of Scottish towns in the fourteenth and fifteenth centuries

More shattering was the utter destruction of casting towns to the flames. The vicious practice of medieval English kings and commanders had manifested itself as early as the thirteenth century when King John, after having been forced to sign Magna Charta, came to Haddington, burnt it to the ground, including the palace, and devastated the surrounding countryside. During the fourteenth century similar vengeance was wreaked on Forres, Kinloss, Elgin, Aberdeen (every building flattened to the ground), Linlithgow and Edinburgh (on two occasions, once including St Giles' Parish Church). Kelso Abbey and Haddington (church and friary) were damaged by fire. Despite the pious endeavours of the English nobility in the crusades to the Holy Land, they felt no reverence for the sacred buildings in Scotland and unhesitatingly destroyed the abbeys of Melrose, Dryburgh and Newbattle. The border towns especially suffered. Dumfries was twice damaged and Kirkcudbright was laid to waste. The fourteenth century also visited on Scotland the revolting member of the clan McWilliam, the 'Wolf of Badenoch', whose band of rebels burned Forres once more, and also Elgin along with the cathedral. These do not represent all

31 Dundee: tower in Fish Street. Houses based on the form of fortified towers in the country were built in some towns in the sixteenth century and provide emphatic features in the street frontages. The relationship of this tower to the country tower houses is evident when compared with Claypotts near the city.

the destructions because many less notable towns and small villages did not escape. The war game was not confined to Scotland for the two nations tended to operate on a 'home and away' basis. Border barons in Scotland needed only to hint at the promise of rich booty to send the Blue Bonnets over the border to seize the English cattle and drive it back to Scotland. Such incursions should have been directed to the demesnes of their real enemies, the powerful English nobles in the south, but they were inaccessible and safe, so the decent northern farmers suffered.

The fifteenth century brought little respite. Military fire-raising destroyed Berwick, Dunbar, Elgin, Stirling, Selkirk (twice), Dumfries (three times), Dalkeith, Blackness, Dumbarton, Roxburgh and Jedburgh (three times).

The sixteenth century and the rough wooing

The sixteenth century witnessed the destruction of Annan (on two occasions, on the last of which not a stone was left standing), Jedburgh, North Berwick, Kelso, Dumfries (four times), Hawick (three times), Irvine, Kircudbright and Lauder (three times), Haddington, Burntisland, Dunbar, Leith and Edinburgh. Towards the middle of the century the Scottish guardians of the child Queen Mary incurred the displeasure of Henry VIII because they had changed their minds about arranging for her to marry his son and heir. Their decision was ostensibly on political grounds. The king, however, had exhibited an alarming tendency to re-marry, putting his former queens to death. It may be inferred that no responsible guardian would wish his ward to be joined with the offspring of such a dubious character, lest what was bred in the bone might have come out in the flesh. But Henry would suffer no one to stand in his way, from Scottish noblemen to his Holiness the Pope. So commenced 'The Rough Wooing'.

In one of the last spasms of English aggression the Earl of Hertford played his part as Henry's hatchet man extremely well, as is now said of cricketers. In 1544 he battered his entry into Edinburgh after he had finished with Leith and systematically had every building set alight, including Holyrood. His troops, working with great enthusiasm, took three days to finish the job. Henry VIII chose his General astutely. His orders for the campaign were to put 'man, woman and child to sword without exception where any resistance shall be made against you'. His further orders were 'extending like [the same] extremities and destruction in all towns and villages whereunto you may reach'. The Earl, after he had had his sport, reported to the king with satisfaction that he had plundered and burnt Edinburgh, Leith, Haddington, Holyrood, Newbattle Abbey, Burntisland and Dunbar, and had stolen 10,000 cattle and 12,000 sheep. He returned the following year when the corn was ripe, not for harvesting but for burning, and his army sacked seven abbeys, sixteen castles, five market towns, and 243 villages. The Earl's personal plunder included the sacred bronze font from Holyrood where Scottish royal infants had been baptised. After adding a scurrilous verse to the inscription he presented it to St Albans. Like the Stone of Destiny, the stolen property was not returned. He was later invested as Duke of Somerset and Protector of England during the minority of Edward VI. This post lasted only two years, after which he was flung into prison and eventually beheaded in 1552.

Life in the burghs from the fourteenth to the sixteenth centuries

Unrelenting fury from aggressors calls for desperate measures from the defenders, especially when they are outnumbered by five to one. During the fourteenth century when attacks were imminent, the Border townspeople were forewarned to gather their cattle and take to the hills, leaving behind only burnt crops. This 'scorched earth' policy deprived the invading armies of food supplies. Their foraging parties were isolated, cornered and destroyed. The supply ships were harried off the east coast, and on one occasion only a single ship reached Leith bearing nothing but the officers' wine. The troops had to be hurriedly led back, dispirited with empty hands and stomachs. Calamities were averted but at a heavy price.

In the fifteenth century war intermingled with famine and several outbreaks of pestilence. In the towns, building was hindered and the markets adversely affected. 'Waste' buildings – ruins – remained for years after they had been left burning, watched forlornly from the hills by the homeless families. It is a matter for wonder that despite the fire and plunder towns regrew in their original forms and the communities revived. Only Roxburgh eventually succumbed and to this day lies beneath the fields with a few stones from its castle protruding above ground. Some other towns may have been partially lost, as at Kelso.

Economic problems unavoidably followed. Devaluation of the Scottish pound had become almost an endemic affliction for about 150 years from the middle of the fourteenth century, when a form of 'monetarism' was imposed calling for restriction on trading Scottish products for foreign goods instead of for currency.

Preparation in the burghs for defence

The austerity laws of 1430 which were instituted to mend the ailing economy restricted not only the ordinary townspeople from wearing fur or coloured clothes below knee length, but also their drinking time in taverns, where time was called at 9 p.m. Football was prohibited under a fine. Bow butts had to be set up, and some of their locations have survived in their names – as at

Linlithgow, Irvine, Montrose, Lanark, St Andrews, Haddington, Annan and Aberdeen. In Glasgow the principal butts were on the Gallowmure, know as the Muir Butts. Others stood at Trumpling and Crackling House Brae near Cathedral Street, and at the Castle.

The sites where possible were to be near parish churches. Later in 1491 golf and other unprofitable sports were also banned. Archery was to be the chief recreation, so keeping the country on a defence footing. Fortifications were strengthened by stone walls and ports round the burghs of Stirling, Dundee, Inverkeithing, Peebles and others in the mid sixteenth century.

In 1490 the Scottish King James IV wrote to the Pope who had asked for money to resist the Turks, advising him that Scotland did not overflow with gold and silver although it abounded in the proper commodities. He added 'our old enemies of England have also harrassed my subjects whom I have protected against the inroads of the adversaries by my assiduous exertions'. One of the measures taken by the king was to enact that the sheriffs' stewards or baillies of the realm were to call for 'wappinschawings' to be made four times in the year. This confirmed an earlier Act of 1425. At these shows of arms or weapons men of between 16 and 60 years were to muster equipped with armour and bows, swords, spears or daggers. In 1491 the people were called upon to practise archery under a penalty of forty shillings for failing to appear. In some places the mark to be shot at was affixed to a building. Irvine arranged for the 'pappingoe' to be placed high up, possibly on top of the tolbooth. The best archer received an award of £12 Scots. Kilwinning placed a similar target on the abbey tower. The area had to be adequate to accommodate one range of about 30 yards (27.4 metres) and a pair, the usual arrangement, needed about 120 yards (109.7 metres), allowing for safety distances behind the targets.

New burghs in the fifteenth and sixteenth centuries

In the latter half of the fifteenth century there were empty sites in many towns such as Edinburgh, and James III gave grants of sites in Berwick to enable re-population to settle where trade was depressed. An additional forty to fifty burghs were erected by barons in the fifteenth century, including Huntly, Kirriemuir, Inverary, Earlston, Wick, Sanquhar, Biggar, Hamilton, Dalkeith, West Linton and Paisley. In the first half of the next century, forty-seven burghs were chartered and in the last half, thirty. Urban growth did not completely stop because of war, therefore, nor did the long periods of instability halt urban life during times when the kings were in their minorities and government was exercised by rival, self-seeking nobles.

Foreign trade

Foreign trade continued through these centuries. This trade called for ships. Some were chartered from abroad, but locally built ships were launched from Inverness, where the long timbers needed could be floated down the Ness from the Highland forests. In the early sixteenth century James IV purchased Newhaven and built the harbour and boat-building yard which turned out the largest and strongest ship of the western world.

Exporting towns such as Edinburgh (Leith), Dundee, Perth, Aberdeen, Linlithgow (Blackness) and Montrose prospered from foreign trade. In the second half of the fifteenth century Kirkcudbright traded with France after the English armies had been driven back to Calais. Earlier, Scotland had gained trade relations with Burgundy. Migration of herring into Scottish waters brought prosperity to the east coast fishing towns and boat-building was revived. Dysart and Preston exported salt, Aberdeen and Berwick exported salmon.

Scotland's trade during the defence of her independence spread over a wide territory. Some of the east coast burghs dealt with Rouen and Dieppe as well as Bordeaux and Rochelle. In the fifteenth and sixteenth centuries trade continued with Norway and the Baltic ports. Scots, especially from Dundee, maintained a colony in Danzig. Many thousands of enterprising individuals journeyed as far as Prussia and Poland. Middleburg became the chief port for Scottish trade, and later the role was played by Bruges. Principally the merchants from Aberdeen and Edinburgh benefitted from this. Finally, in the mid-sixteenth century Campvere wrested the position as Scotland's chief staple port on the continent.

The whole trading activity introduced to the burghs luxury goods, and foreign countries influenced the quality of town life and building. French master masons were attracted to Scotland. The character of the burghs accordingly related more to the experience of Dutch or Flemish towns than to those of their near neighbours in England(**32**, **33**).

The Scots became accustomed to travel from these early times. At the end of the fourteenth century Sinclair sailed to the Faroes, and the Earl of Orkney reached Greenland and possibly America. A Scot became an abbot at Ratisbon, and there were Scottish student colonies and professors in the French universities. This enterprising alacrity to journey wherever duty called was to become a national characteristic in many spheres of life.

Education

By the fifteenth century most Scottish burghs had organised grammar schools. In the earlier centuries Church schools had

32 East Wemyss. The harmony of materials, scale and colour placed in informal groupings typifies the burghs in the East Neuk of Fife.

33 St Monance. The harbour frontages contain only four elements: the broad sweep of the water; the strong harbour wall; the stretch of house fronts; and the sky. There are no ornaments, trees or hills. Only the church, very properly, and a few roof lines appear above the frontage. Terracotta pantiles, some slates, varied light-coloured walls, Georgian windows and broad dark doors are the simple components, but the picture they produce always gives delight.

predominated, teaching plainsong and Latin. Scholars would also have received teaching in arithmetic. An Act of Parliament at the end of the fifteenth century required all barons and well-to-do freeholders of land to send their eldest sons and heirs at eight or nine years of age to school to learn Latin, and thereafter to spend a further three years studying art and law. The cathedrals also ran grammar schools and by the end of the fifteenth century were expected to turn out boys with perfect Latin. Prior to the founding of St Andrews University in 1411 students received their education at the famous seats of learning in Padua, Paris, Orleans and Avignon. Cambridge and Oxford were less attractive to Scots who needed a guarantee of safe conduct – so these universities were denied many brilliant students. Glasgow University was established in 1450. Between 1495 and 1505 Aberdeen had two universities – as many as England had. Edinburgh University was established in 1582. The buildings had stone walls and displayed an unmistakeable Scottish character. The teaching was classical, comprising logic, Aristotle, rhetoric, analytical study, dialectics, philosophy, physics, astronomy, ethics, metaphysics and the mind, meteorology, perspective, arithmetic and geometry.

It is of interest that the son of James IV, who became Archbishop of St Andrews, studied under Erasmus. He held the young Alexander in great esteem for his diligence and his aptitude not only for his chosen subject, but also for his general learning in rhetoric and Greek and his talent as a musician. The Scottish Court under the Stuarts at that time was one of the most cultured in Europe and led Scotland in its Golden Age of learning. Later this attribute of the Stuarts brought the legacy of fine paintings and art to the National Galleries and Collections.

The musical teaching in schools, however, tended to decline. By the end of the sixteenth century a lack of school buildings was being felt in small towns and parishes. The level of schooling in the burghs was demonstrated by the fact that although writing was not a common accomplishment in either Scotland or England, many in Scotland could write. Signatories of documents in a burgh like Inverness, remote from the centre of the country, signed by their own hand. They included watermen and fishermen who could be regarded as average townspeople.

Recreation and spectacle

Despite the turbulence of the times, sport, recreation and festivities were not entirely excluded. In the sixteenth century the hammermen in Perth played football on the South Inch. Play was robust. 'A's fair at the ba' at Scone' including broken limbs, apparently. The hammermen decreed, however, that their apprentices must continue work while they were playing.

Glasgow paid for six footballs at Shrove Tuesday celebrations. Candlemas was the scene of a colourful ceremony at Aberdeen, where the craftsmen processed through the streets in a prescribed order according to their crafts, from the fleshers, barbers and bakers, shoemakers, skinners, coopers, wrights, hat makers and bonnet makers to the fullers, dyers, weavers, tailors, goldsmiths, blacksmiths and hammermen. Each craft had a part in the performance of the play 'The three Kings of Cologne', a medieval legend still popular in the sixteenth century and apparently an annual event in many burghs.

At Court pleasure was given by musicians, dancers, circus performers and jesters. In Edinburgh and Dundee touring English drama companies were welcomed but probably not entirely appreciated because of the differences in dialect. Great displays were witnessed in Edinburgh at the marriage of James IV and Queen Margaret in 1503. A painted gate and towers were erected in the High Street with singers representing angels. The richly-dressed participants processed to meet the royal couple and followed them chanting. A newly-painted cross was erected, and a fountain ran with wine. A stage showed the three godesses, Paris and Mercury, and another a religious tableau. A second gate contained the four Virtues, and on the way musical instruments played. The town was hung with tapestries. Lords and ladies, gentlemen and gentlewomen watched from every window and great throngs lined the route while the church bells 'rang for mirth'. High Street with its ample width and high buildings, much referred to by visitors at the time, provided the most fitting background for such pageantry.

The rise of stone building in the burghs

As the seventeenth century approached, stone building in some burghs began to take over from timber construction. The most important buildings, such as tolbooths, became prominent, incorporating civic accommodation, gaols and even shops. Edinburgh's tolbooth of 1560 was given over to a gaol. Other examples were erected in Canongate (1591, four-storeyed with shingled roof), Dysart (1575), Musselburgh (1590), and Peebles (1572). Perth's handsome hospital was built by James VI. James V brought in French masons for new works at the palaces at Linlithgow, Stirling, Falkland and Edinburgh. St Andrews has some stone university buildings dating from this period, and it is likely that small houses with stone vaulted ground floors began to be erected. Inverkeithing also had at least one stone-vaulted house in the sixteenth century(**29**, p.61). The stone College house in Elgin dates from 1557. Stirling's two attractive turnpike-fronted houses at Spittal Street were built during the sixteenth century(**13**, p.34). Also, 'Darnley' house is an excellent example of a house of three storeys with vaulted ground floor and dormer windows. In Edinburgh, notably, Baillie Macmorran, a rich merchant, built his house to a standard fit for a king, and James VI and his queen attended a banquet there in 1593. Even in Irvine, Roxburgh House is known to have had a panelled interior with wide stone fireplaces. A much earlier house dating from the early fifteenth century, Sklate Hall, had a slated roof and probably stone walls. The rising demand for stone is indicated by the granting of permission to open a quarry there outside the town.

The gradual introduction of stone for the external walls of

houses took place for three likely reasons. First, quarrying techniques were improving because of the use of gunpowder for blasting and the skills that had been acquired by sappers and military miners in the undermining and blasting of castles – an early example of the use of war-time technology for peaceful purposes. A more important reason for the use of stone, however, is that serious fires were beginning to occur where timber buildings in towns were becoming closely built together (**7**, p.20, **34**). Even in the fifteenth century fire had destroyed buildings in Stirling (twice), Linlithgow, Cupar and Aberdeen. Town legislation soon prohibited timber frontage galleries, and timber forestairs were to disappear. Finally, timber was becoming scarce in Scotland on account of the overfelling of trees, difficulties in transporting timber from the Highland forests, and the use of wood for fuel over many generations.

Horticulture

In the last half of the fifteenth century James III gave to the Greyfriars in Glasgow ground with a garden attached. The Bishop of Glasgow laid out an orchard near his palace, as did the prebends around their houses. As well as gardening, the great abbeys pursued animal husbandry, bee-keeping and wine-making.

Townspeople were also keen gardeners, benefitting from the knowledge and the plant specimens of the monasteries. Also, the shortage of timber was becoming obvious to the more enlightened landowners. The tenants of Sir James Pringle, for example, were compelled to grow trees. In the sixteenth century tree planting in the back gardens of Aberdeen was so intensive that approaches to the city gave a view of a town built within a wood.

The decline of the monasteries

At the end of the sixteenth century an essentially medieval constituent of Scottish towns was to expire. The religious orders had in most instances gone into decline, and no longer served as centres of religious guidance and teaching, or of sound practice in cultivation and husbandry. In 1559 John Knox descended upon Scotland like a vengeful Ayatollah. The thunderous indignation of his sermons up and down the country fired the fervour of his congregations, who surged upon the monasteries and sacked them. As in mobs throughout history there were those whose acquisitive urge far outweighed their religious zeal. The monasteries in Perth were first to be sacked, and Knox was quick to follow up with further sermons at important towns such as Dundee, Scone, Stirling, Edinburgh and Linlithgow. But what Knox later admitted was rascal multitude were not the only pillagers. By subtler and less conspicious means the landowners

quietly annexed the buildings and lands and destroyed the buildings by studied neglect and quarrying. Thus what the English Lord Hertford had started, Scottish zealots continued and Scottish thieves finished. In a short phase of reckless destruction the towns lost the cream of three hundred years of Scottish architecture. In 1587 Queen Elizabeth ordered the execution of Mary Queen of Scots, maintaining the reputation of her kinsman Henry VIII. In 1603 James VI left for England and the Scottish royal burghs lost their close relationship with king and court.

34 Edinburgh: Bow Head, High Street, 1852. The celebrated Bow Head Corner, demolished by the town council in 1878, was the most fascinating example of the many timber-fronted buildings in the city. By 1852 some of the mouldings and other features had been removed, but the bold technique of the carpenters in the oversailing of each floor survived to the end.

5 The Seventeenth Century

New burgh charters
Over 160 small villages were elevated to burghs during the seventeenth century but few developed. Those which thrived included Bo'ness and Grangepans with their salt pans and harbours, Thurso(**35**) with its harbour, Greenock and Port Glasgow as major ports to the west, Leadhills for lead production, Stornoway and Campbeltown with harbours, Methil exporting coal and salt, Moffat and Langholm. Also belatedly, Leith, after centuries of being suppressed and exploited by Edinburgh, received its burgh charter(**XV**).

35 Thurso: Shore Street. Another urban scene of simple ingredients disposed on a plan with a nicely judged turn at the focus. Gabled ends and a fat, old turnpike tower projecting into the street appeal to every discerning Scot.

The beginning of manufacturing industry
The specialisation of towns did not occur to any extent during the seventeenth century, nor was manufacturing yet competing with the dominance of the marketing of goods as the chief commercial function of burghs which still relied on the countryside for their products. However, a few indications of the approaching industrialisation in Scotland appeared, especially in the west. Greenock set up factories for fish-curing and soap-making. Glasgow was prominent, introducing sugar refining, coal mining and the manufacture of paper, soap, cloth, rope and hardware. Tobacco, brought from America despite the determined efforts of English rivals to prevent it, was also

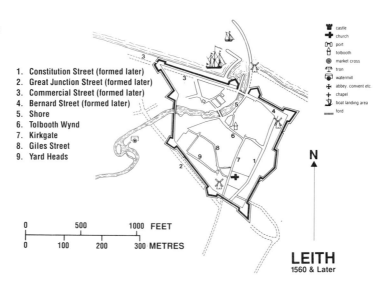

Map XV Leith, 1560 and later. Leith was the only town in Scotland having defences designed on the continental model. They were erected by the French but were soon demolished at the request of the townspeople. The siting of the fortifications, however, later determined the location of the perimeter streets.

1. Constitution Street (formed later)
2. Great Junction Street (formed later)
3. Commercial Street (formed later)
4. Bernard Street (formed later)
5. Shore
6. Tolbooth Wynd
7. Kirkgate
8. Giles Street
9. Yard Heads

castle
church
port
tolbooth
market cross
tron
watermill
abbey, convent etc.
chapel
boat landing area
ford

N

LEITH
1560 & Later

becoming an important commodity. In 1635 the merchant-dominated town council established a woollen factory in an old manse in Drygate, an early example of a building being converted to new use. This was later incorporated into a larger concept for manufacture and retail. By the end of the century three companies were employing 1,400 people producing wool and linen cloth. A silk weaver was granted freedom from public burdens for five years by the town council, which later established a silk-dyeing workhouse (1682).

Between 1667 and 1700 four sugar-houses were built in peripheral situations in Candleriggs, King Street, Gallowgate and Stockwell Street. Machinery was imported from Holland, waste molasses was used for distilling rum. Other industries on the city's edge included ropeworks on Glasgow Green (1696) and glassworks just north of Broomielaw (1700).

In other burghs companies ventured into glass-making, potteries, and the production of gun powder. Cotton manufacture made impressive progress before the end of the century. Edinburgh had a foundry, Leith had a sawmill, and Glasgow was preparing to smelt metals. In most cases new industries needed new or altered buildings, especially in the case of rope works where long narrow rope walks had to be provided. The most conspicuous buildings in the Scottish burghs were the windmills, an alternative to water mills where the source of power sometimes stopped due to hard frost or the summer droughts. Leith had three massive stone mills designed by Robert Mylne in 1685. Other known examples were at Montrose (three mills), Aberdeen, Berwick, Forfar, St Andrews, Glasgow (at Gorbals), Dundee and Edinburgh.

New industry needed then, as now, finance. A Scot founded

the Bank of England in 1694. In 1695, at the suggestion of an Englishman, the Bank of Scotland was set up.

Functional divisions within the burghs

By the seventeenth century the functions of various quarters in towns were generally established. The important markets occupied the best central locations. The showing of horses and the display of timber needed the larger space for manoeuvring beasts and the long lengths of imported timbers. The flesh markets where meat was cut up were frequently located off the main market-places in vennels with a good slope for drainage. The separation of market functions included many trades such as salt, leather, shoes, oats, meal and seed, fish(**25**, p.55), butter, cheese, skins and lime. Nearly all of these open market functions were maintained into the nineteenth century, to be replaced by covered wholesale markets and the modern forms of merchandising.

Trade also tended to concentrate where houses were located: in Edinburgh, for example, there were silversmiths and goldsmiths in the Bow Head(**34**, p.76) and Old Parliament Close(**36**). Tanners worked near water on the outskirts of towns, as at Edinburgh (Tanfield), Dundee and Stirling. Tallow makers were isolated because of the noxious fumes and fire hazard.

Town dwellers began to distinguish the desirable from the undesirable locations for building houses. The very poor or persons of ill repute, street cleaners, tanners and midwives (who were not accorded much respect) often lived on the leeward side of a town, near noise and odours. In the quarters favoured by

36 Edinburgh: Old Parliament Close. This late eighteenth-century drawing shows St Giles, the parish church of the burgh and the flat-roofed shops which ranged along High Street and were occupied by jewellers, goldsmiths and watchmakers. The artist gives a satirical view of the daily life from which no one escaped – from the judges, the military and the merchants down to the fishwives, sweeps, beggars, pickpockets and entertainers.

37 Edinburgh: High Street and Tron Church. The tall, narrow frontages have been inherited from the widths of the twelfth-century plots of the burgesses. The street follows along the top of the ridge which falls away from the castle rock in a long glacial tail down to Holyrood. The gap was made in the late eighteenth century to make way for the North and South Bridges. The Tron Church was built in the seventeenth century to relieve the parish church after rapid population growth.

successful townsfolk, back gardens were maintained and proximity to a royal palace was regarded as an advantage – as at the foot of Canongate in Edinburgh, or Broad Street in Stirling. Where the medieval plots had been built over, the most sought after houses occupied the street frontage, or the bottom of the plot where the view was more open.

Churches and tolbooths

New churches were built at Dairsie, South Queensferry, Anstruther (Easter), and Burntisland early in the century. Later, the Tron church was erected in Edinburgh(**37**). Many churches suffering from war damage needed expensive repairs – for example, St Giles in Edinburgh(**3**, p.10), South Leith Parish Church, St Nicholas in Aberdeen and Glasgow Cathedral.

The century saw the expansion of the tolbooth accommodation: Glasgow acquired a five-storey steeple(**38**) and Aberdeen a tolbooth of five-storeys. Other towns where tolbooths were built or extended include Culross, Dingwall(**39**), Inverkeithing, Kirkcudbright, Linlithgow(**40**), Maybole, South Queensferry, Wick, Rothesay and Peterhead. Some were later enlarged, or demolished.

Trade halls

Various trades became incorporated towards the end of the fifteenth century, and by the seventeenth century they had built

38 Glasgow: Tolbooth Steeple. Although now in a totally unsympathetic setting, the impressive tolbooth and market cross bear witness to Glasgow having been a great civic power and leading commercial centre in the eighteenth century and nineteenth century. The city continues to generate new enterprise.

or acquired premises for their meetings in some towns. Only a few buildings have survived: in Edinburgh, the Tailors' Hall (1621), the Hammermen's Magdalen Chapel (mid-sixteenth century), and Candlemakers' Hall (1722). Shoemakers' Land (1785) still stands in Banff, but in the nineteenth century other fine buildings were demolished, such as the Trades Hall in Dundee.

The standard of living in towns

Education for children improved during the century. Graduates were in charge in many of the Lowland schools, and Latin was taught. Nearly all the established burghs had schools which were not neglected by the councils. In Edinburgh and Glasgow the pupils received a thorough grounding in Latin, working long hours under strict discipline, and were required to speak only Latin in the school and playground. Education of girls was less formal, but some were sent to private establishments. The simplest schools took pupils from the age of five who were given a five-years' course of eight hours for six days a week. The pupils learned to read and write and were taught Scripture. Even in the middle of the previous century the town school curriculum at Montrose included Scripture, French, Latin, grammar, Horace, Virgil, Cicero, Erasmus. There was also recreation: archery; fencing; swimming; wrestling; athletics and golf. By the end of the seventeenth century the country's education system was in advance of that in England and most countries in Europe. As well as the High School, Edinburgh had English schools, French schools, reading and writing schools and a fencing school.

School buildings had to be improved and many towns were engaged in the work – such as Dumfries, Peebles, Dunfermline, Rothesay, Peterhead, Montrose and Kilmarnock. Also during this century the Advocates' Library was founded in 1682, and

39 Dingwall: High Street. This clean, bright shopping centre, which sets off the character of the burgh buildings, is being wrested from the motorist and given back to pedestrians.

40 Linlithgow: the Cross. The frontage of High Street was broken to form a fitting location for the imposing civic building with its great staircases, façade and tower. In front stands the ornamented well in the form of a crown. Behind, the open spire sits a little unconvincingly atop the tower of the parish church. The square leads to the royal palace.

the Royal College of Physicians in 1681, both in Edinburgh. At this time an Observatory was also planned for Edinburgh but not built, but the Exchange was completed before the end of the century. The new Parliament House was also built.

The disapproval of the Kirk in Scotland did not stop the opening of Edinburgh's first theatre in the middle of the seventeenth century, but it was soon closed. After a period of closure of all theatres, Allan Ramsay opened one in 1736 – but it was closed within six months as a result of the Church's antagonism. Theatre in Edinburgh began to develop again after the middle of the century, but Glasgow's Playhouse was burned and destroyed by fanatics.

Townspeople had a great choice of goods available in the shops: they could buy virginals, fans, ostrich feathers, harp strings, pearls, spectacles, thimbles, tobacco, whisky, wine, prunes, walnuts, chestnuts, anchovies, caviar, caraway seeds, drugs, silk, spice, furniture, alabaster dolls, rattles, guns, armour, swords, glass and sponges. The wide variety of goods available caused new shops to open in the towns. In Montrose, for example, a wig-maker started business, and powder for wigs was obtainable.

Emigration and trade

During the seventeenth century Scottish influence spread abroad. About 50,000 Scots settled in Northern Ireland, and there were about 30,000 in Poland, England and the Baltic. The 'Dugald Dalgetties' of Scotland made up 10,000 men in the battalions of Gustavus Adolphus, and some rose to the rank of Lt.-General. The flair of the Scottish professional soldiers proved to be the salvation of Britain in the Napoleonic Wars – as Pitt acknowledged in the House of Commons when he deflected some of the praise given to himself by pointing out that it was his idea to call upon the fighting qualities of the Highlanders. It was not simply as rankers that these Scots contributed: a small island like Harris alone provided scores of generals, colonels and officers. Scottish generals and an admiral also served in the Imperial armies of Russia.

The Civil War depreciated trade in the burghs. Commerce with England ceased and Scottish merchant ships were harrassed by English privateers. Edinburgh suffered, Aberdeen merchants lost their ships and cargoes, and bankruptcies followed.

Later in the century, despite the two countries being united in one Kingdom, an imbalance in trade was maintained against Scotland by about one-third exports to England and two-thirds imports from England. Scottish overseas trade was meant to complement that of England, but not compete. Scotland had no Navy, exporting to Europe was hazardous, and English wars with Holland stopped Scotland's trading there. The English merchants intended also to organise a monopoly in trade with North America, but the business thrust of Glasgow's merchants outmanoeuvred their English rivals and so ensured the rise of the Glasgow tobacco tycoons.

Towards the end of the century Scottish ports were receiving timber from Norway, iron from Sweden and flax and hemp from Danzig. Importation of wine, fine textiles and manufactured goods also arrived on the east coast. Bo'ness, Port Seton and Methil exported coal from the expanding coal fields, even under the Forth at Culross, including 60,000 tons to London. The richer merchants of Edinburgh began to invest overseas in enterprises in France, Spain, the Canary Islands and Danzig.

Supervision of building

In the course of rebuilding in earlier centuries it was apparently not unknown for an unscrupulous owner to steal out at night and adjust a fence or march stone to his better advantage: 'Cursed be he who moveth his neighbour's landmark', says the Prayer Book. Then it was that the liners, and later 'comprisers of biggings', were called in to check and, if proved, correct any misallocation or unsatisfactory construction. In later times the Dean of Guild and his court would call for a report from the liners on any question of doubt about boundaries. As the sixteenth century approached, this function of the court extended to the control of the details of building, such as the positions of lean-to additions affecting neighbours, or the heights of chimneys to prevent smoke and fire. Restrictions were imposed on the use of timber at entrances, and ultimately the use of timber for external walls and thatch for roofs was prohibited. The courts were also concerned to ensure that adequate accesses were maintained for buildings, and that middens and garbage were promptly cleared away. Even questions of allowing sufficient sunlight and daylight into rooms in houses were subjects of deliberation. In order to regulate such matters every building owner was required to seek the court's approval before proceeding on alterations or new building. The concept of development and building control was therefore regarded in Scotland as an essential element in burghculture.

Measures against fire were seen to be critical following serious conflagrations in Edinburgh, Dunfermline, Irvine and Glasgow.

But despite the adoption of the regulations the old timber buildings endured and serious outbreaks of fire occurred into the nineteenth century.

Gardens

The cultivation of gardens for urban pleasure and need was prominent in the seventeenth century. Early in the century the gardeners of Glasgow became an incorporated trade. Advances in the varieties of plants, gardening lay-out and techniques improved the gardens of the time, and Scottish successes in horticulture resulted in the export of fruit trees abroad.

In Edinburgh, Canongate was particularly rich in the gardens of its sequestered closes. And the seventeenth-century garden of Regent Moray is reported to have been 'of such elegance, and cultivated with so much care as to vie with those of warmer countries'. Pear trees, a weeping thorn and remains of elm bowers survived until 1829(**41**). The first physic and botany

41 Edinburgh: Regent Moray's Garden, Canongate. This famous garden, with the thorn tree planted by Mary, Queen of Scots, was still maintained in 1829.

garden in Edinburgh was begun in 1670, and shortly afterwards Reid's two volumes of the *Scots Gardener* gained a wide reputation for the gardeners of Scotland.

Population growth and congestion

As burghs slowly prospered they expanded by the penetration of additional houses down the plots behind the frontage buildings. The process may have begun to develop more quickly in the last half of the previous century. Early indications of it appear in Braun and Hogenburg's Map of Edinburgh in 1582. In less than 100 years the map produced by Gordon of Rothiemay, although impressionistic, contains evidence of areas in the city where ground behind the front buildings was built over to saturation point. The policy of packing in houses in depth behind the front property set in motion a significant new shift in the evolution of burghculture. The development of building upwards by incorporating several storeys also began about the end of the sixteenth century, and Edinburgh's example was followed by nearly twenty other towns in varying degrees(4, p.15).

Sport

Racing was well established in Leith Sands by the middle of the seventeenth century, and meetings also took place at Cupar, Lanark, Hamilton and Irvine. These were sponsored by the king, especially by James VI. Substantial money prizes were put up. The races were run over eight miles, twice round the circuit at Irvine and four miles at Leith. The events usually ran yearly and brought enthusiasts from all over the country. In the early nineteenth century the Leith course was transferred to Musselburgh, and for a further short period resumed on the Sands from 1836 to 1856.

Leith Links was also one of the first golf links. James IV and John Knox are said to have played there, miraculously to relate, on a Sunday. In the sixteenth century the game was prohibited during the time of preaching or sermons, and later it was totally banned on Sunday by Edinburgh town council. Musselburgh also became a home of golf.

Cock fighting became popular as coal mining expanded. Mining seems to induce in the underground worker an absorption with natural life to compensate for working in an environment which does not support life. In Tranent, the oldest mining town in the country, the men reared game cocks for their fighting qualities and held competitions matching their birds against others – local and from other towns. Cock pits existed in Leith and in places such as Dalkeith, Macmerry and Elphinstone. The sport was eventually prohibited in 1844.

Manly sports in the small towns and villages included wrestling, weight throwing, and quoits, for which a site was reserved at Leith Links into this century. Bowling and tennis were known, but the latter seems to have developed extensively only in the eighteenth and nineteenth centuries.

Pestilence

Plagues affected the burghs during the seventeenth century. Bubonic plague, brought by a ship from the continent, broke out in Leith and spread into the countryside. About twenty percent of the population perished, probably because their resistance had been reduced by food shortages. In Leith the dead numbered more than the living. Part of the Links was made into a mass grave as the cemeteries became full. Ruthless measures were needed to control the situation. One rascal who attempted to take over a property when the owner had died was found guilty, tied to the Tron and a notice put on his head declaring his crime. His tongue was then held by forceps and 'run through with a hot iron or bodkin'.

The famine which affected the whole of Britain at the end of the century after four consecutive harvest failures hit some of the remote parishes so severely that about half the population starved to death. Nevertheless, the country had enjoyed about thirty-five years of freedom from famine from 1660.

Population growth was thus retarded in the seventeenth century, and prosperity in the burghs suffered, leaving Scotland in an impoverished condition.

6 1700-1830 and the Second Age of Town Building

The regeneration of Scottish thought

At the beginning the burghs had grown out of three constituents: a market-place, a church, monastery or abbey and a castle. They were dependent on the countryside with its agricultural production and in many cases on a harbour, which was in some important instances located in an associated town beyond the burgh.

As time passed the relevance of the monasteries declined and by the end of the sixteenth century had been extinguished. At about the same time the introduction of gun powder and seige guns also reduced very considerably the function of the castles. During the seventeenth century it began to be evident that the merchants did not need to live close to the market, and thus houses could be separated from the chief place of business.

By the middle of the following century Scottish life was transformed in a sudden rapid process of expansion. The nation experienced a release of the spirit first entering and seizing a few receptive intellects. In turn, other minds became activated so that expectancy and imaginative thought began to energise all aspects of living. The educated Scots, long good Latinists, seized the opportunity of putting into practice the ideal balance and restraint of classical art. Their native practical approach to life directed them towards the employment of machinery and the useful application of theoretical ideas. The change transported Scotland into a new age of economics, finance and eventually insurance. The production of power was multiplied many times as the ingenuity and discoveries of engineers and chemists were pressed into transport, manufacturing and engineering. Wealth increased, and the population grew. The chain reaction of a new urbanculture which spread across the country began and advanced in pace with the expansion of the intellectual forces.

It would be fair to assume that when the first burghs of the twelfth century grew up and prospered, thought and learning flourished. Christian teaching was central, influencing art, music, architecture and writing. The practical affairs of commerce, agriculture and husbandry were also undergoing change. Surviving, records are meagre, but it was in Scotland that Michael Scot, born near Kirkcaldy, became a man of science who acted as astrologer to the Emperor Frederic II (1194-1250), and his reputation spread throughout Europe and lasted for several centuries. At the same time new engineering techniques were being introduced in building and water power. The next renaissance over five hundred years later was again motivated by a new inspiration in the age of rationalism and science. Its earliest intimations showed before 1700 in many spheres of learning such as in the mathematical work of Napier, extended and developed by members of the Gregory family, Maclaurin and Stirling into the eighteenth century. This point is made only as an instance of mathematical advance, but similar equally revealing examples could be made in respect of the natural sciences, astronomy, meteorology, chemistry, geology, engineering, zoology, oceanography, botany, agriculture, geography and exploration, medicine, dentistry, actuarial science (a Church of Scotland minister introduced life insurance for widows and orphans in 1743), political economy, psychology, landscape and portrait painting, literature, poetry and architecture. In such a ferment of intellectual dedication it would have been odd if urbanculture and town planning had stayed dormant. It happened, however, that town expansion was in demand and another impressive age of Scottish town making had arrived by 1750.

The craftsmen and builders

Craftsmen concerned in the building of towns and known to have been practising in Scotland in the twelfth century included blacksmiths, masons and wrights. The craftsmen in the following century were not content to remain in an inferior position in the burghs. They sought to attain burgesship and succeeded. As they had been firmly under the control of the king and merchants who prescribed prices and quality, the crafts formed themselves into guilds for their own protection. By the end of the century relations between the factions became strained. However, the craftsman under the rules of burgesship could not trade abroad unless he gave up his trade. By the end of the fifteenth century towns were admitting the incorporation of trades such as the masons and wrights, and the hammermen. This concession conferred the right of craft incorporations to participate in the election of magistrates.

The rules that governed the guilds or incorporations required that entrants to the craft had to serve seven year apprenticeships and pass examinations entrusted to selected master craftsmen such as masons and wrights of recognised skill. In the seventeenth century the test for wrights included the requirement to draw and set out details of buildings, such as a panelled niche or a three-light Venetian window. General designs may have called for plans of a large house, say 100 × 50 feet (30.48 × 15.24 metres) on plan, and of several storeys complete with staircase and balusters. Special emphasis was placed on the principles of Palladio. These facts demonstrate that these aspiring apprentices were being prepared for the

42 Dumfries: Castle Street and St Thomas Church, nineteenth century. An example of how the classical sense of balance and refinement was introduced into Scottish burghs in the Georgian period.

profession of architecture as well as master craftsmen. It explains how Robert Smith as a joiner and member of his guild could emigrate from Dalkeith to Philadelphia in the mid-eighteenth century and assume the role of a classical architect whose work still survives to demonstrate the degree of his accomplishment. It is probable that other young master tradesmen found their way into the offices of the architect sons of well-to-do families in the seventeenth and eighteenth centuries to produce designs and architectural details for which they would never receive recognition. These architects, however, were likely to have taken some part in the work of their offices apart from seeking and meeting clients and organising business and finance, unlike some of the architect businessmen of the twentieth century. It is understandable that classical grounding of general education and apprenticeship should have manifested itself in the harmonies of production and refined detail of even the humblest eighteenth-century and early nineteenth-century buildings(**42**).

The new form of town planning: the towns in north-east and south Scotland

Even before 1750 urban forms new to Scotland, such as squares, were being built in Edinburgh by forming open courts across the width of several medieval plots. Brilliant innovations in village planning were introduced at Gifford in East Lothian and in Inverary in Argyll, where the introduction of three-storey flats followed the established tradition of urban living(**XVI**).

The most influential impetus towards the new planning was

Map XVI Inverary, seventeenth–eighteenth century. A compact classical small town which offers a graceful aspect as viewed from Loch Fyne.

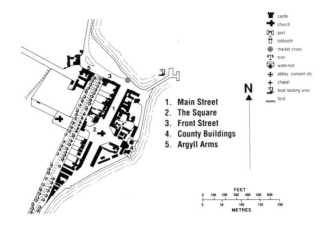

castle
church
port
tolbooth
market cross
tron
watermill
abbey. convent etc
chapel
boat landing area
ford

N

1. Main Street
2. The Square
3. Front Street
4. County Buildings
5. Argyll Arms

FEET
0 100 200 300 400 500 600
0   50   100   150   200
METRES

INVERARY
Seventeenth & Eighteenth Centuries

Map XVII Keith, eighteenth century. A neat, logically planned town where the stiff lines of the streets are relieved by attractive variations in the stone houses which front them. All the houses conform to the building line except for badly placed recent rebuilding.

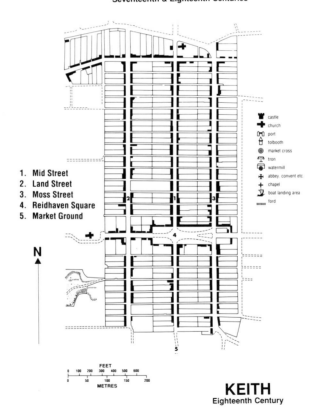

1. Mid Street
2. Land Street
3. Moss Street
4. Reidhaven Square
5. Market Ground

castle
church
port
tolbooth
market cross
tron
watermill
abbey. convent etc
chapel
boat landing area
ford

N

FEET
0 100 200 300 400 500 600
0   50   100   150   200
METRES

KEITH
Eighteenth Century

first given by Keith in Banffshire(**XVII**). This plan was prepared for the Earl of Findlater by Peter May in 1750, and the success of the venture was quickly perceived by other landowners. The layout of the streets in Keith seems certain to owe their arrangement to the native medieval plans which, as has been shown, consisted in essence of a central street or market-place

43 Keith: Reidhaven Square. Keith was one of the first eighteenth-century New Towns. The square was intended as a large market for trading, cattle sales and so on. The simple designs of the houses, of up to two storeys, the use of stone and slate and the strict adherence to the building lines produced a clean, orderly town.

about 100 feet (30.5 metres) at its widest part. Flanking this street were the long plots of the townspeople which terminated at back streets or cowgates. The ends of the main street or market sometimes were marked by a castle, abbey or open ground. Vennels connected the market street with the cowgate. Following this example, the eighteenth-century town designers embodied the pattern in the new plans. The lay-outs varied in detail, as at Aberchirder and Fochabers, or more radically in the cross plans of Stuartfield and Newmill: Fetterangus and Mintlaw had market-places respectively oval and diamond shape. At New Deer the main street was planned to focus on the church, and to be divided by a square at the middle.

Peter May's plan of Keith provided a main street, Mid Street, extending about two-fifths of a mile (1.61 kilometres) in length (**XVII**). Moss Street and Land Street were set off parallel on either side of Mid Street, which at about half its length was furnished with Reidhaven Square, a spacious open area used for trading and fairs(**43**). The object of the promoters was to take advantage of the nationally famous fair held annually on adjacent land. They wished also to promote the linen industry in the town. An hotel was built and two churches were eventually established, one of which is a splendid perfectly sited classical edifice with a dome(**44**). A tolbooth and gaol were planned and shops, although not seemingly identified at the planning stage, appear gradually to have been incorporated. The agricultural basis of the early burghs was still implied in the first plan where stables and byres were built in some of the long plots with access on to the cross lanes. Stables were maintained well into the first

44 Keith: Reidhaven Square and St Thomas Church. The New Town plan allowed for this splendid little domed church to lie on the axis of one of the shorter roads leading from the square.

half of this century. The freedom of individual action permitted within the broad control of the plan resulted in a diversity of houses, buildings and people which are essential to the social and commercial elements of urbanculture.

The tree-lined leys outside Keith formed the Common. In many of the towns which followed this example the owners made similar additional tracts of land available on the outskirts for the villagers or townspeople to cultivate, and to gather peat, lime and stone, conforming to the policy adopted in medieval planning. Enthusiasm occasionally over-reached practicality and some village and town plans had to be abandoned, or were only partly built. But many succeeded. The development of a style in art evolves from pure and uncomplicated beginnings towards ever more fanciful and intricate forms(**45**). Town planning does not escape this progression, as the plans of some of the nineteenth-century villages demonstrate. Circular streets were adopted for the village of Longside: St Fergus had elliptical roads, Strichen and Friockheim adopted triangular street plans, and a hexagonal plan served for Wolfhill village. Other places tended to degenerate into gridiron feuing plans in which their creators did not exercise any artistic imagination, not so much because they chose not to, but because they did not have any to exercise.

Outstanding examples include Monymusk, replanned in 1776 beside its ancient church around a grass area, and at the end of the nineteenth century skilfully 'Tudorised' by the feudal superior in a delightful style. The Earl of Eglinton promoted the extension to Eaglesham in 1770, a magnificent gesture in planning(**XVIII**). Central to the scheme is the 200-yard-wide (183 metres) grassed area with a central tree-lined stream running down a slope for about one-third of a mile (0.5 kilometres). At about the centre a textile mill was built with a 45 foot (13.7 metres) diameter water wheel. The architecture of the houses over the years has been transformed and enriched, reflecting the fashion and style of the passing years, a splendid

45 Edinburgh: Royal Circus. A typical example of the many monumental street designs in the capital's New Town.

Map XVIII Eaglesham, eighteenth century. This boldly planned layout earned much praise in the eighteenth century and still provides an attractive place to live.

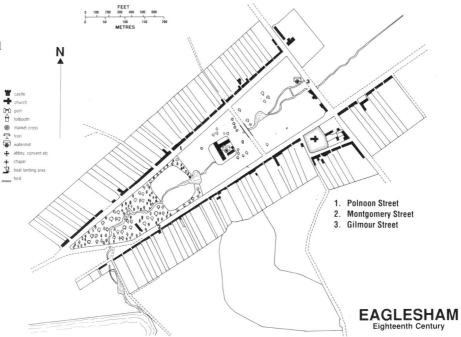

N

castle
church
port
tolbooth
market cross
tron
watermill
abbey. convent etc
chapel
boat landing area
ford

FEET
0 100 200 300 400 500 600
0 50 100 150 200
METRES

1. Polnoon Street
2. Montgomery Street
3. Gilmour Street

EAGLESHAM
Eighteenth Century

46 Eaglesham. This is the most spacious eighteenth-century town in Britain. Some of its houses have been modified and altered, giving a mixture of styles and ages. Still, the great central open space of grass, shrubs and trees remains.

example of how planning should be exercised(**46**). Unlike the grand opera of the planned frontages of some of the cities, the practices in the small towns produced the architectural variety shows to which everyone, apart from architectural purists, can wholeheartedly respond. It is little to be wondered at that at the end of the eighteenth century travellers used to refer to Eaglesham as one of the most delightful places in Britain.

Urban geometry supersedes organic planning

Although eighteenth-century towns derived their form from the twelfth-century burghs, the planners did not accept that the site conditions of slope and physical features which mould and shape the surface should affect the plans. Influence lines where they existed were ignored. For surveyors, planners and architects the strict geometry of the 'T' square and set square was the new controlling force. The planners assessed the possibilities of the site on the ground, and then returned to their chambers to draw out on paper the layout of every street, square and lane. They followed the approach taken to draw out a plan for buildings. For practical reasons regular walls parallel and at right angles to other walls have been followed for individual buildings since medieval times. This approach, however, was not regarded then as desirable or necessary for town building. As has been shown, the medieval planners set out the town plans on site, modifying the outlines to suit physical conditions. However, it would have been difficult for eighteenth-century minds disciplined by a rational ordered approach to life to see any virtue in allowing

47 Edinburgh: Princes Street. Princes Street evolved from dull eighteenth-century frontages to the pulsating sweep of late nineteenth-century façades. The opulent gradeur and stylistic inventiveness of Jenners department store characterises the street at its zenith.

the anarchy of untamed nature to interfere in an organised system of streets and squares. Thus Scotland was led into a lengthy period of town building which followed strictly set straight lines and where the direction of the first street dictated the lines of the adjoining streets in running exactly parallel, irrespective of the gradient or cross-falls as at Cullen, for example. This approach was only modified long after the policy had been questioned in 1813 by the perceptive mind of a young Edinburgh architect, William Stark, who lamentably died 'too young to have done much'. He pointed out that the harmony and measured allotment of streets, squares and crescents 'was of little consequence . . . except upon paper'. He alone among his contemporaries seems to have been aware that the line of streets should be determined by the contours. Accepting such methods, planners would set out streets which might cease to be straight, but would gain 'in a bending alignment . . . much beauty, and perhaps the most striking effects'. Stark illustrated the underlying fallacy by analysing the symmetrical geometry of Craig's 'New Town' Plan for Edinburgh.

Craig's plan for Edinburgh's first New Town
Designed in 1767, seventeen years after Keith, Craig's plan embodied the traditional form of a main central street on a slight

48 Edinburgh: Heriot Row. The palace façades of Heriot Row and Abercrombie Place facing south across Queen Street Gardens provided elegant living for the well-to-do in the eighteenth century and nineteenth century. Many of the addresses are still dwelling houses despite commercial competition.

ridge, with squares at either end extending overall to three-fifths of a mile (0.96 kilometres) between the opposite ends of the squares. This street, George Street, was flanked on each side by two lesser parallel streets, Princes Street(**47**) and Queen Street. The traditional town lay-out was elaborated by three cross streets and a system of minor parallel streets which pass between the main streets. From Stark's point of view the enjoyment of the spectacle of George Street did not depend on the existence of Princes Street and Queen Street, or whether or not these were parallel to George Street. Whether Charlotte Square and St Andrew's Square were equal or different in dimension carried no reference to the appreciation of the spectacle as seen by the pedestrian observer. Nevertheless, this basic illogicality of approach does not detract from the impressive quality of the plan as a setting for façades and stately focal buildings, and it affords great pleasure to Scots to know that the plan was directly descended from the urban native ancestry and not from some French idea cribbed from a book.

The tyranny of the drawing board ultimately dominated the architecture. Whole street frontages were drawn out to represent

49 Dundee: Reform Street. This was an enlightened response to improvement by a Dundee council in the Georgian age of town building. Reform Street could still flourish if a new town council would arrange for a uniform treatment of painting, the proper alignment of the shop fascias and the prohibition of projecting shop signs.

50 Glasgow: Terrace at Great Western Road. The terrace shows skilfully designed ends. In creating classical compositions, Glasgow's architects and planners showed a warm exuberance and superior professional talent.

51 Cupar: St Catherine's Street. The street is a classical addition to the historic centre. It succeeded because the scale of the new buildings was not allowed to dominate the smaller scale of the older buildings.

symmetrical elevations like single palaces. At first the long frontages between the cross roads in Princes Street and Queen Street in Edinburgh were designed as a series of houses with similar windows and uniform heights, but were not elevated to the palatial pretensions of a single building. In Heriot Row(**48**), Great King Street and Royal Terrace in Edinburgh, in Reform Street in Dundee(**49**), and in the later streets in Glasgow(**50**), Perth and Cupar(**51**), the full combined lengths of the frontages were designed as complete balanced façades, although the intended effect may not always be discerned immediately from the pavement in front. If the architects had been thinking of the buildings as a street and not as a drawing board creation, the result might have differed. These palace-like frontages extend to 600 feet (182 metres), and even up to 1200 feet (365 metres). This monumentality is maintained in the heights, for the ceilings are eleven feet (3.35 metres) to thirteen feet (3.96 metres) and two, three or four storeys are distributed through many of the streets, for some in Edinburgh incorporate four-storey flats.

The houses in the main streets in the new areas were reserved for the well-to-do. Shops were thought to be too vulgar for inclusion, and although some of the less wealthy could obtain small houses in the back streets, the lower orders were left in the older out-of-fashion parts of the old town.

Edinburgh's New Town and modern urban social theory
The new areas represented segregation with large blocks, wide streets, squares planted with grass, or, as in Drummond Place, first used as cab parks. Residential human scale was deliberately ignored. Densities in terms of people were not low, for many households had large families and all had domestic servants living-in. By 1865 Craig's New Town, with many shops, churches and so on then introduced, had a gross density of 90.3 persons per acre (223 persons per hectare). This gross density was drastically in excess of the 60 persons per gross acre (148 persons per gross hectare) of the modern city's Wester Hailes district, regarded by social scientists as one of the best areas to enjoy their favourite game of social pig-sticking. In the flats in Frederick Street families in the top flats had about seventy steps to climb to reach their houses. There were no front gardens.

The modern theorist of urban social science will recognise these vast, large-scale eighteenth-century housing schemes – with their huge communal gardens (such as those in Queen Street, Edinburgh) and their long, broad, often empty streets – as a sort of place where individuals and small groups of neighbours would be deprived of their right to control their own territory and enforce civilised behaviour. Modern social theory insists that in such places residents are bound to feel threatened, helpless, deprived, neglected and under-privileged (or possibly over-privileged). Such places are always found to be awash with litter and the walls covered with graffiti. Thus it is proclaimed from the high places of academe. But this calamity has not occurred in the 200 year-life of most of the Scottish classical housing schemes – or if it has, history has kept quiet about it.

The theories emanate mostly from study of English experience. Scotland has a longer tradition of flats, houses without front gardens, higher ceilings, and even multi-storey flats. Flats in seventeenth-century and eighteenth-century Edinburgh reached up to fifteen storeys. More significantly, residents of the classical areas in cities and towns were generally of equal status with a common civilised outlook. Only regressive people make slums; progressive people prevent them.

The deficiencies of classical planning

Because new planning in the cities was directed towards housing the wealthier citizens, it differed fundamentally from the objectives of the twelfth- to thirteenth-century town planning. When in the seventeenth century the councillors in Edinburgh received an offer from James VII of ground beyond the city, it was intended for the building of a complete capital city to take the place of old Edinburgh, which was to be abandoned on its hill like Old Sarum. This ambitious proposal lay far beyond the vision of Edinburgh's council in the mid-eighteenth century. Their new building and the landowners' later extensions were truly prodigious in mass and breadth, but were inadequate in appreciation of urbanculture. At the outset the city extensions of the planners did not take in commerce or industry. But the forces of commerce started to take the extensions over. One new house in Queen Street in Edinburgh was used as a lawyer's office from the beginning and was never lived in. Small shops such as perfumers began to appear. Residents resisted, but the high prices paid to purchase houses and put them to commercial use apparently overcame the scruples of more and more owners. In the first New Town shops had been opened in nearly all the principal streets towards the east end by 1800. Some shops had also penetrated Hanover Street, Frederick Street and even George Street. On the north side of Princes Street eighteen shops occupied the street-level rooms, and the small frontage on the south side contained three hotels.

The number of commercial premises was still growing in the 1830s. Four more hotels were added and more shops and offices with greater variety ranged along the east end as far as Frederick Street, with the consequence that influential residents retreated to the more exclusive addresses in Charlotte Square, or to those being developed farther west. In 1850 shops occupied most of the ground floors in Princes Street, and by the end of the century only one complete house, owned by a lawyer, was still

52 Glasgow: Park Terrace. A confidently designed building in an area where the city's classical planning excelled.

occupied as a dwelling house.

In Glasgow the first classical westward streets, as well as George Square with its fine residences, came into the hands of commercial promoters from the middle of the century. As in Edinburgh, newer, exclusively residential areas were built beyond – at Park Circus, Park Terrace(**52**), Crown Terrace(**53**), Woodside and Royal Circus. Driving onwards regardless of gradients, the Blythswood area was also laid out and built on a grid plan, but it too was infiltrated by commerce even before it was completed.

53 Glasgow: Crown Terrace. The sweep of the colonnade at Crown Terrace again emphasises the wide vision of Glasgow's designers in the classical period. They were designing streets and their environs, not merely buildings.

The objective in the eighteenth-century and nineteenth-century cities was not a balanced comprehensive city plan but a narrower policy – the fulfilment of the desire of the privileged minority to live in elegant surroundings. Shops, offices and factories did not need to have elegant environments, nor did those who worked in them. Therefore no classical architects were needed, and no plans were made for houses for the less wealthy or for commerce. Their implantation in cities was haphazard until speculative building in the later nineteenth century laid out large areas of tenements for the tradesmen and workers necessary for the survival of cities. In comfort and appearance the quality of the buildings varied, but recent stone cleaning and renovation vividly demonstrates that they have more character and style than most critics in the past were prepared to admit. Stone still makes the most telling contribution to the character of Scottish cities. The not undignified façades should be compared to the mean monotony of the closely regimented dark brick rows of the English mill towns of the same period.

The old town centres and their neglect

The new extensions, superb architectural achievements in themselves, created cultural disaster at the heart of the cities. The leaders in the new movement recognised how the new areas helped to achieve a form of classical idealism, but they seem to have been unresponsive to the qualities of the old town centres. Nowhere was this more manifest than in Edinburgh. Half a millennium of the civic life of Scotland's capital from birth to maturity had been bred into what Geddes described as this

54 Edinburgh: Back Close, Cowgate, 1850. The sturdy stone-walled houses were later extended by timber projections on which further projections were progressively added up the face. These often made charming internal features in the rooms.

Back Close — Cowgate
10 June. 1850

55 Edinburgh: Riddle's Close, Lawnmarket, 1854. An example of two courts with dividing arch between, fitted originally with an iron gate. Here from the sixteenth century lived Baillies, Provosts, Lords of Session, and a King and Queen banquetted. The planning is highly skilled, the architecture Scottish and of good quality.

56 Dundee: St Margaret's Close. The plan, based on a series of courts linked by covered passageways or pends, creates in the perspective an intriguing sense of expectancy.

'labrynthine civic complex'. It had grown and evolved with its people. There was no other city that so patently reflected its nationhood. If the vernacular in architecture is the expression of native character in architectural terms, then the old town of Edinburgh was the vernacular city in urban terms. With natural facility, generations of tradesmen had taken stone, timber, slates and tiles and raised them up high on the side of the ridge in a most astonishing and varied fashion. They seldom departed from the lines of the twelfth-century closes. Each range of building that extended back from the building on the front street was consequently very near to its neighbours. Sometimes they curved slightly to conform to the bends in lanes or closes between. The blocks also incorporated some projections or set-backs. Most astonishing were the cantilevered portions above, supported by ornamental stone or timber beams and brackets, nodding across the close to another opposite so that neighbouring occupiers came almost within touching distance (**54**).

There was little symmetry(**55**). Diversity in layout introduced small intimate courtyards; cross building, at the entrances to closes and along their length, produced the pends beyond which the daylight and sunlight invitingly beckoned the visitor. Dundee had a similar example(**56**). When the slope of a close became

58 Edinburgh: Chalmers Close, High Street, 1860. Some garden ground, rarely found elsewhere in the High Street, still survived down this close at the time of the drawing. The close opened up a view to the north towards Princes Street. The feature of projecting a room extension on the top floor was used frequently in other closes and was one which Sir Patrick Geddes introduced into his own home at Ramsay Garden.

steep, broad steps were provided. Outside stairs gave access to first floors(**57**) and turnpike stairs branched off with doors often set at an angle looking towards the close entrance, providing a natural direct access from the public way(**58**). Sometimes a close would stop at a single-storey house built across it.

All this was accompanied by a rich repertoire of urban architectural detail: splays; stone corbels(**55**); moulded stone string courses; generous Scottish moulding round the doors(**55**); lined window shutters at ground floor; simple ornamental lamp brackets; great chimneys often rising in different widths from the ground with corbels and set backs(**59**); crowstepped gables; lean-to additions; octagonal and circular turnpike stairs with thistle, rose or fleur-de-lis finials as a typical international gesture; stepped buttresses; timbered walls rising from stone walls; vertical, horizontal and diagonal boarding; canopies with carved wooden brackets; stone and wood carved Latin inscriptions; armorial bearings; tympan gables; clothes-drying poles and washing lines conveniently stretched diagonally across the closes(**58**); massive or small stoned rubble walls; stone cellars; dovecotes hung on the walls; rabbit hutches; free-run poultry; window flower boxes; classical pilasters; medieval shaped arches; small window panes; broad astragals(**60**); weather cocks; decorated chimney pots; timber fronts with horizontal windows

57 Edinburgh: West Bow. One of the most picturesque streets in Europe, West Bow was utterly destroyed in the nineteenth century.

59 Somerville's Land, Lawnmarket. This sixteenth-century timber-fronted house, characteristic of its time, marked the junction of Castle Hill and the Lawnmarket. The three dormer gables rise with the slope of the street, growing in stages like the three bears. The house was demolished by the Free Church of Scotland to make way for an extension to the College.

60 Edinburgh: Netherbow and John Knox's House, *c.* 1760. The town gate or port dividing Edinburgh from Canongate was demolished as a serious road obstruction. Sir Frank Mears made a design for a restored wide-arched port as the city's monument to Edward VII, but the palace yard statue was preferred.

divided by narrow mullions(**34**, p.76, **59**); a rustic classical piazza; a timber bridge across a basement area; stone flags; cobbles; stone slabbed roofs; Scotch slates; some red pantiles; and roughcast and wooden lathed timber walls.

This spectacular architectural switchback progression of hundreds of closes and vennels all branching from the contrastingly wide streets, and set high above the surrounding landscape was native Scotland. Edinburgh's New Town straight and restrained stood coolly below, a stranger in the land.

There were some who may have had doubts about the new order. Hamilton, the romantic classicist, must have had some sympathetic feelings for the neglected old city, for he could hardly otherwise have drawn the elevations of the Lawnmarket, Castlehill and the Bow with such care and industry. Yet even he was ready to demolish much of Castlehill and the Lawnmarket to replace them with what would have been a poor improvement scheme. James Drummond and Bruce J. Home, Victorian artists, faithfully recorded in accomplished sketches what still remained in their times. Sir Patrick Geddes well understood the deep wrong being done to Scotland in the old cities and recognised their sad neglect at the end of the nineteenth century. Single-handed, he took practical steps to arrest the decline, even electing to reside in the Old Town. Bruce J. Home referred to

Knox's House & Netherbow Port, circa 1760

109

the demolition of the Old Bowhead in 1878(**34**, p.76) as a calamity, wantonly occasioned by 'the vandalistic actions of their existing civic authorities', and pointed out that 'not many cities have suffered more than Edinburgh from this cause'. In Glasgow, J. Pagan in the 1880s deplored the losses in Gorbals village of the old landmarks, and he cautioned against overcrowding by Irish immigrants: 'When once tenanted by these modern Huns', he wrote, 'the destruction of the fabrick is not far distant'.

The clearance of Edinburgh Old Town by fire and demolition

The Old Town buildings in Edinburgh did not decline solely because there was an epidemic of *anorexia civitatis* in the City Chambers. Much earlier, in 1700, about one-quarter of the city suffered devastation as a result of fire, and in 1824 a large area again was burnt down and many buildings were demolished — one by explosion when the mines were touched off at a countdown at noon precisely on the day of the fire, an event dramatically recorded by the lightning sketches of a newspaper reporter of the time.

There is no doubt that the towns which suffered from overbuilding of the old closes faced what must have appeared to be by 1850 an insuperable problem. The answer must have seemed clear cut: if bad conditions were giving offence to the community, remove them by removing the buildings. Some had the correct approach even during the first half of the century. An Edinburgh man, Dr Foulis, took a close in the Grassmarket, gutted it and repaired it inexpensively, cleaned it, and made comfortable houses for the poor. They were taught cleanliness and supervised, and any not susceptible to the lesson, after patient trial, quickly had to leave. The close stood out as an oasis amidst wretchedness and filth. Yet the example was not followed.

Obviously in most cases the severe congestion of houses would have demanded some careful extraction and opening up. But if a wise plan of adaptation could have been achieved — keeping some closes and clearing some adjacent less worthy buildings at intervals — conservation and urban renewal would have coincided. In his plans for the tightly packed areas of houses in Indian cities, Geddes had applied such techniques, which he described as 'conservative surgery'. Some recent restoration work has also adopted the principle.

Little now survives of the vennels and closes in Scotland's towns. In the small towns the buildings in the closes were simple but pleasing, as may be judged where they can still be seen(**61**). The closes of Edinburgh were not merely a string of flat elevations. In these narrow ways the frontage presented an almost incredible confusion in recesses and projections of bold

61 Jedburgh: Blackhills Close. An excellent example of restoration of a close with its parallel rows of houses, each built down the former garden of a medieval burgess plot.

solid geometry. This home-produced bewildering manipulation of geometric shapes in glorious disorder was the perfect antithesis to the flat, calm regularities of the ordered elevations inspired by ancient Rome in the architecture of the New Town.

Eighteenth-century and nineteenth-century roads

Growth of population and the expansion of towns during the second half of the eighteenth century called for better means of communication over the country. Telford, more than just one of the foremost engineers of his day, supervised an integrated road system mostly in the north of the country, complete with over 1,000 bridges, some of advanced design and striking appearance. The Lowland roads were also undergoing improvement based on J. L. McAdam's specifications, and by the end of the eighteenth century the coaching age had become established. Fast stage coaches and good roads between towns needed straight, wide and direct routes through towns. The historic narrow, restricted accesses to High Streets and market-places were subjected to increased demands of vehicular traffic. Down came the last of the medieval ports(**60**). The mercat crosses, seen as useless encumbrances, were dismantled and either resited or thrown aside. New roads were driven through or across the older street system. As roads in the planned burghs were usually from the outset built on generous lines, the call for

111

total clearance fortunately did not arise. In Edinburgh the North Bridge cut through High Street, and later George IV Bridge also bisected High Street at the foot of the Lawn Market. Edinburgh Road and South Street were driven across High Street in Dalkeith. Similar coach roads were provided in Lanark and at George Street, Princes Street, Methven Street and Tay Street in Perth, Tower Street and Ettrick Terrace in Selkirk, Church Street and Buccleuch Street in Dumfries. The demand for coaches benefitted Edinburgh, where the first vehicles employing modern assembly-line methods were produced and exported to London and Europe. The new roads are still recognisable by their uniform widths and straight direction. The zeal for building new roads to bisect the main streets took such a strong grip in Perth that the typical linear form of the city was changed into a gridiron plan, with further cross streets at the broader King Edward Street duplicating Meal Vennel, and at Scott Street. The policy at the time created a net increase in street building frontages and allowed building promoters to produce more tenement flats. It did not promote traffic movement or road safety, as was recognised a century or more later. The improved roads hastened postal services. Williamson of Edinburgh seized the opportunity to provide the new service of a penny post for letters. This grew so rapidly that the Government was obliged to buy the business and extend it to become the Royal Mail – perhaps the earliest act of 'deprivatisation'.

Canal building
The beginning of the coaching era coincided with the development of canal building. The case for building canals was being energetically canvassed. Smeaton in 1764, reporting on the proposals for the Forth and Clyde Canal, had asked: 'If the ancient Egyptians, Greeks or Romans had been acquainted with the use of locks, or the Chinese, the French or the Dutch, would they have so long neglected an opportunity furnished and pointed out by nature for so great an improvement of the commerce and policy of the country?' Scotland did not have to wait so long as the Egyptians, but delays postponed the completion of Smeaton's canal until 1790. Together with the Monkland Canal, it served Glasgow for heavy bulk movement of coal and iron. The cross-country link for shipping quickened the pace of growth at Grangemouth and less directly, Leith and Falkirk. But by the middle of the century railways had thrust their lines over the country and canal traffic rapidly declined.

The start of modern industry, 1700–1800
From about the middle of the eighteenth century the manufacture of textiles began to influence urban growth and

change. First there was linen. In 1725 fine linen and thread were being produced in Glasgow and Paisley, the spinning first accomplished by hand looms. The trade possibilities of textiles were perceived over the country and the object of landowners in the north-east, east and south-west of Scotland was to establish textile mills and build villages and small towns to attract both mill owners and labour. The mills in Clackmannan eventually produced nearly one-quarter of Britain's wool requirements. Such enterprises needed organisation and finance, for which the British Linen Board and the Linen Bank were established in 1746.

Scottish inventors, geologists and chemists entered the world of manufacture, producing dyes at Perth in 1753: green from copperas and lichen, purple from cudbear and other colours. In 1749 Prestonpans was making vitriol for the bleaching fields, which had to be located near plentiful water supplies. The newspapers of the time carried advertisements by bleachfield owners bringing to the notice of manufacturers the availability of their service. In 1780 Watt improved the French process using chlorine and Tennant made further advances in 1798.

The cotton industry, 1780–1830

By the end of the century cotton production was enthusiastically pursued by manufacturers. The first water-powered textile mill was installed in Penicuik, on the brisk flowing river North Esk. Rothesay made headway in water power, and the cotton boom grew in Paisley and East Kilbride, Johnstone and other towns. David Dale, with Arkwright's assistance, set up a mill at New Lanark which employed over 1,300 people. The village was also built with tall stone tenements, like the mills, but producing the other essential to cotton spinning, children and adults to do the work. Dale's exploitation differed from that of other captains of industry because of the benevolent philosophy of New Lanark's proprietor, Robert Owen. The survival of New Lanark was ensured in recent times when, on the initiation of Lanark Burgh, Sir Frank Mears and Partners were asked to advise on the future planning. Now, after years of restoration and conservation, New Lanark survives as a model nineteenth-century Scottish mill town, and as a witness to Owen's 'co-operative socialism'.

The cotton era generally declined by about 1830. Water power ordained the positions of the mills at the outset, but the rapid introduction of Watt's improved steam engines at the end of the eighteenth century freed industrialists to locate their factories at points accessible to coal, and later to the new railways and towns with large populations. The concentration in central Scotland starting at the end of this period and based on coal and mining determined the population spread of modern Scotland in the central belt.

Coal production, 1750–1830

The extraction of coal began to increase after 1750. Explosives were used to speed up the sinking of the shafts at Penicuik and the Lothians. Coal had been in use for many centuries, but when its suitability for iron processing was discovered demand grew, and for some time coal was imported from Newcastle. Work in the new pits was dangerous, but the miners were held by the masters under a lifetime agreement. If a worker tried to escape the masters advertised the 'offence' in the newspapers, warning others not to give him any gainful work that would maintain his livelihood. Vagrants were forcibly recruited into the system. The men hewed the coal but did not carry it. That duty was left to women and children, male and female, from the ages of five or six years. The women bore the coal up ladders about 70 to 100 feet high (21–30 metres) and along passages from 100 to 400 yards (91–365 metres), carrying from one to two hundredweight. The shift would last for twelve or thirteen hours. Sometimes harness was used for carrying the coal on the bearer's back and neck, or it was hooked to a sled or wheeled bogie, the women often having to crawl on hands and feet on inclines of 1:3 to 1:6(**62**). When bogies were introduced the 'bearers' became 'pushers' and took their loads downhill to the shaft bottom to be lifted by a horse-gin, a procedure less burdensome than carrying the coal to the surface. The women continued to have large families – ten or more – and permitted themselves only ten to twelve days off work at each birth. It was known for a woman to come up and go behind the slag heap to have her baby in the open field. The face miners had an average life of 45 to 50 years, but those who drove through sandstone seams died (with severe lung infections) on average at between 35 to 40 years. The children helping the women went below each winter day at 5 a.m. and came up at 6 p.m., so rarely ever seeing daylight in much of winter. This happened at a time when the lives of the intellectual privileged were being dazzled by the brilliance of the Enlightenment, but the lives of those who laboured with their hands were being eclipsed in the blackout of outrageous social injustice.

Tranent and other mining towns naturally became shabby and dirty – like the inhabitants who could not attend church because they had no clean clothes. The blackened houses above stood on areas of ground covered in grit from the slag heaps, a scene which one observer likened to 'greasy old hulks stranded in a sea of treacle'. Digging gardens could not provide recreation for miners after twelve hours of digging coal.

62 Women and children drawing hutches in coal mines. In the eighteenth century each woman carried from one to two hundredweight of coal in a creel on her back up ladders to the surface about thirty times a day. In 1808 the work was condemned as 'severe, slavish and oppressive in the highest degree'. In 1843 an Act of Parliament prohibited the worst practices.

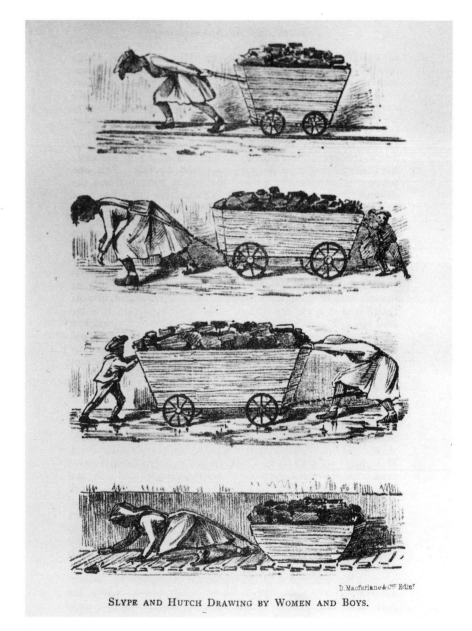

D.Macfarlane&C?.Edin?

SLYPE AND HUTCH DRAWING BY WOMEN AND BOYS.

Iron production

Iron processing developed with the Industrial Revolution. The Carron Works at Falkirk expanded, producing carronades and rails and items for the building boom. As the nineteenth century progressed other centres grew, especially Coatbridge, which led in iron production over much of Britain. Other iron producers set up works at Wilsontown, Dalnotter, the Clyde Iron Works, Cleland and Muirkirk, all centred around Glasgow. Sixteen blast furnaces existed before the end of the century. The coal and iron age altered the old pattern of the traditional burghs, strategically positioned to promote commerce and form an economic unit of agriculture and urbanculture. Now, the new centres were placed in areas unconnected with the countryside, and sometimes detrimental to it. The presence of coal, ironstone and transport were the only factors governing the choice of site. By 1830 the population in the industrial parishes in Lanarkshire was doubling, and the towns of Coatbridge, Motherwell and Airdrie were set on course for rapid growth to come.

The traditional industries and new institutions

The traditional industries were expanding to meet the needs of the growing population. Agricultural produce had to supply the milk, meat and grain for the Lanarkshire and Ayrshire workers. Crieff and Falkirk flourished as the Scottish centres for beef cattle before their export on hoof to Smithfield, the cattle being shod to withstand the journey. Brewing at Edinburgh, Alloa, Glasgow and Dalkeith expanded where water supplies were pure. The rebuilding and new extensions in the towns called for vast quarrying projects for building stone, granite, whin and slates. Timber was imported, and metal components such as nails, screws, hinges, locks, grates and iron pipes were being made in quantity. Lime, sand, fireclay chimney pots and pipes, and glass were in demand throughout much of the country.

The modern paper industry became established in Penicuik, Polton, Fife, Aberdeen and Glasgow, using woollen rags and esparto grass imported into Leith and other ports. The printing trade grew in Glasgow and Edinburgh, from Ruddeman College Printers early in the eighteenth century to the production of the first British Encyclopaedia in 1768–71. The growing taste for reading led Allan Ramsay to start the first circulating library in Edinburgh in 1725. Earlier in 1691 Crieff had been the first town to start a public library. By the end of the century Edinburgh had become a leading centre of book production, and Scottish printers and booksellers were breaking the London monopoly. By 1754 Glasgow was making its intellectual contribution by setting up the Glasgow Academy of the Arts. The Royal Academy in London was established fifteen years later. Also in this period, the new observatory was built in Edinburgh to replace the earlier one of 1776, and the Royal High School was completed. In the 1840s Glasgow and Perth were assembling collections for city museums.

Classical serenity and industrial thrust

In the course of 130 years the direction of Scottish life changed in three ways – ways which were both inter-related and conflicting. The countryside assumed a new importance because of the need for increased agricultural production, but whole rural parishes were absorbed into towns, cities and industrial sites and agricultural land was bisected by roads, railways and canals. The intellectual life of the times opened up the mind to new vistas of culture and understanding but seemed to blind many thoughtful persons to the horrors of industrialism and social injustice. Finally, the great work of building the classical towns, symbols of culture and refinement, was being resisted and was finally halted by the competing demands of the captains of industry.

Industrialism had created problems. It was in the hands of a minority whose single-minded aim, with few exceptions, was to create vast wealth for themselves at the expense of the welfare of others. The failure of Scotland to achieve industrial progress without social and urban decline can be blamed on both those at the top of society who lacked the will to rectify the problems, and probably also on the absence of a direct Parliament to enact the necessary legislation.

7 The Later Nineteenth Century (1830-1900)

The Scottish Baronial revival
In the latter half of the nineteenth century many architects began to realise that the Scottish element was missing in architecture and the Scottish art of town making had lapsed. They reacted by decorating their buildings with turrets at the corners of the streets and carved pediments on dormers – details which had been banned by the classical purist architects of the previous century. Scottish mouldings to doors and chimneys and crow-stepped and ogee gables came back into fashion. Although the style emerged from enthusiasm for national ornament, it no more succeeded in producing an authentic Scottish building than could be produced by draping tartan over Salisbury Cathedral. Moreover, the layout of streets too often merely degenerated into a drawing board solution of obtaining the maximum number of houses on a piece of land shaped in accordance with the fortuitous boundaries of ownership.

The Victorian contribution to the High Street
The burgh High Streets underwent a significant evolutionary change in the latter half of the nineteenth century. If there was a characteristic which distinguished Victorian architects from their predecessors, it was in the individualism of their buildings. They felt free to design in any style – not just classical or baronial, but Gothic, French, Florentine and Queen Anne. They also delighted in appropriately ornamenting their façades. For street corner buildings they would splay the corner or add a gable or circular turret(**19**, p.42). Dormers were welcomed(**39**, p.83). Oriel windows and bow windows indicated a superior dwelling or office(**63**). To be very grand they pushed up the scale to let their building dominate its neighbours, they threw in columns, pilasters, cornices and entablatures.

These innovations succeeded because architects conformed in two respects. They retained the sash-and-case windows, taller and larger than those of the seventeenth century, and not necessarily classically proportioned like those of the Georgian period. But the windows kept their family connection. The second choice they made was to continue the important tradition of using stone. Exercising these practices the Victorian architects rarely put a foot wrong. They made their way about the main streets in the cities or the small burgh High Streets neatly inserting their worthy buildings – from the splendid palaces of commerce in the cities(**64**) (especially Glasgow), to the tenements

63 Renfrew: the Burgh Chambers. A romantic assertion of civic importance is symbolised in the centres of administration designed by Victorian architects for many of Scotland's burghs.

with shops and banks in the small burghs(**27**, p.58). As their building usually conformed to the narrow width of frontage left by the removal of an earlier building, they also complied with the historic 'module' set by the burgesses' plots of the twelfth century. A potent reason why some present century High Street buildings fail to please lies in the failure of their architects, some very distinguished, to observe the 'module' as an essential element of Scottish traditional urbanculture. Indeed, some modern architects even emphasise their disregard for it by slashing continuous horizontal windows and shop fascias from end to end of the longer frontages.

The location of industry

Before the middle of the last century it was being discovered that towns no longer consisted of only houses, churches, shops and the tolbooth. Towns began to need mills, factories and engineering works. This happened when these plants were being forced upon the burghs by promoters who would suffer none to obstruct them. They admitted no evil in noise, smoke, smell or ugliness. Such incidentals were regarded by the proud owners as symbols of prosperity. Some towns achieved a satisfactory solution by concentrating industrial buildings in areas naturally screened from the town – as at Selkirk, or Penicuik. Others segregated them at railway or canal terminals, or in river valleys. The less successful locations occupied the vacant sites on the perimeter of towns that happened to be available at the time of building, without thought to future building and extensions, and regardless of their position in relation to wind direction or neighbourliness. However, nineteenth-century indifference to the planning of industrial sites and railways furnished later

64 Dundee: In the mid-nineteenth century the city built a series of streets to the north of the medieval town, each lined with handsome building radiating vitality. The skilful turning of the corners of the architecture at the street junctions shows that the architects were thinking in terms of streets and not merely of the buildings themselves.

generations with the strongest evidence in support of town planning and the art and science of urbanculture.

It was acceptable to locate any type of industrial building anywhere in a town or city except for those streets intended to be reserved for superior residences. With this exception, all forms of industrial development were unopposed. In amongst the tenements, shops, hospitals and schools there appeared builders' yards, scrap yards, breweries, warehouses, rag-stores, flour mills, distilleries, metal founders, tanneries, printing works, glass makers, slaughter houses, knackers' yards, light and heavy engineering works, manufacturers and railway marshalling yards. Ship builders and chemical works occupied sites on or near the coast in seaside towns.

In the industrial areas of towns and cities soot, fumes and dust from industry mixed with the effluent from the chimneys of thousands of household fires and grates. Black columns of coal dust rose high above the ports when ships were being coaled for boiler fuel or export. The polluted air blackened the new stonework of tenements, and penetrated to lace curtains and household linen. Workmen came home with grey faces, and the women in the factories working among pitch and chemicals turned a permanent pale yellow. The unreality of the atmosphere at the steel workings lay over the individual boom towns in the west: yellow clouds by day and pillars of fire by night. In Edinburgh's Princes Street artists portrayed the castle rising above a Romantic Scotch Mist in the gardens below – produced by the steam and smoke of the busy railway lines at the foot of the castle. A century or more later, the practice is to segregate industry from the residential parts of towns, while modern technology has made it possible to eliminate industrial air pollution and noise, and the new attitude towards architectural design and landscaping has made many modern industrial buildings compatible with those in residential areas.

The railways in towns

Railway promoters foresaw the superior advantages of railways in serving equally well the transport of goods and passengers. There were no close rivals. The driving of the lines into the very heart of the cities was essential. Suburban lines were also seen to be a profitable and popular service. Railways branched out to dominate the cities before most other civic considerations. The planned expansion of Edinburgh was abruptly halted and railway routes cut across the land earmarked for suburbs in the process of construction. The fine planned expansion of Edinburgh towards Leith was progressing until the railway lines laid an obstacle across its path. The railways made it possible for cities to expand laterally by producing a fast service from suburbs into the business centres and across to industrial areas, but they reduced the amenity of contiguous land, especially at depots and marshalling yards. The lesson had not been learned in the last century that when new forces of urban change are seen to be threatening the naturally evolved pattern of a city, they must be modified in order to gain the maximum benefit with the least harm. Also, if at any time, no matter how inevitable, a revolutionary change seems to be for the better in the evolution of a town, its immediate dominance will eventually decline and be superseded by something else. Not only did the nineteenth century fail to learn these lessons: recent urban road schemes have resulted in urban incongruities.

From an engineering point of view the new Scottish railways were competently planned. Tunnels, cuttings, embankments, bridges and viaducts did not impose too severe a penalty on the countryside – unlike the present day motorways. The problem in the cities and some towns arose because the criteria for the suitable siting of lines greatly differed from the traditional road lines. Influence lines in pedestrian and horse vehicle movement had no meaning for railway engineers. They did not in any case run the track down the streets, as was done in American towns. But the engineers did drive and bore their way into Princes Street Gardens in Edinburgh – the next best thing. Various rail companies wound their systems round the then perimeter of cities, penetrated into the minor centres, and set out sidings wherever space permitted. The developments were not planned as parts of towns or cities, they were driven through in spite of existing roads and houses. Land was used up profligately, often merely duplicating the tracks of other companies. In the Gorgie district of Edinburgh lines and sidings criss-crossed and sliced up an area of ground equal in size to the whole of Edinburgh's New Town. Portobello was effectively cut off and encircled by lines and a massive marshalling yard. Perth, traditionally a communications centre, was seized upon by the railway companies who blocked off a large part of the south-west of the town from natural access to the town centre. The Dundee line passed at high level along the backs of the fine Georgian houses in Marshall Place, and left an unsatisfactory road junction at St Leonard's Bank. In Linlithgow the main line running along the edge of the medieval burgh left only one good road to connect the town with the land to the south. If the railways in towns and cities had not been superimposed, but controlled and treated as means of serving the towns as an element of urbanculture, towns and cities would have evolved without the internal conflict of railroads and residences. If railway development had been controlled in this way, it would have been more economical of land and money.

Retreats from Victorian cities

Railways did more than make it possible for people to live in the suburbs of cities such as Glasgow, Edinburgh and Leith and Dundee and work at a distance from their homes. They also permitted the more affluent businessmen to live in towns as much as 22 miles (35.5 kilometres) away. Towns such as North Berwick were popular for Edinburgh and Leith, and Helensburgh was virtually created for the prosperous city men in Glasgow. Both towns were then terminals. The trains were instrumental in bringing top men in commerce and industry together twice a day more conveniently than a club. One powerful figure in Leith would even order an engine with driver and fireman, a guard's van or guard and a single first class coach to take him to North Berwick if he missed his evening train – for he would not be seen in his frock coat, silk hat and gold-topped walking stick left behind, even in a first class waiting room. One other respected Victorian commuter from North Berwick could be seen in his corner seat engrossed in his morning paper, which few knew concealed a penny dreadful recounting the exploits of the hero who employed a fictional flying machine which had a versatility in advance of its counterparts of over a century later.

These men built large villas on their own grounds, from which a coachman would convey the master to and from the railway station. The building plots could be about 165 feet square (50.3 metres) equalling 0.62 acres (0.25 hectares). The larger plots reached two acres (0.81 hectares). In Helensburgh the town has roads 60 feet wide (18.28 metres) set out on a grid and is on a south-facing slope rising up from the banks of the Clyde to an elevation of over 100 feet (30.5 metres). Spaciousness and tree planting compensate for the stiff geometry of the layout. These pleasantly situated towns evolved as residential retreats for the cities because the railways made it possible.

Spas and hydropathic hotels

Preoccupation with matters of health has frequently characterised peoples' activities in history. The Romans relaxed and reinvigorated themselves in hot and cold baths. The medieval people sought to cleanse the spirit which affected their physical well-being by going on pilgrimages. Health farms and rest-cures respond to today's needs.

In Europe the vogue for taking the waters in the eighteenth century and nineteenth century was followed in Scotland. In Peterhead a well believed to have medicinal properties was discovered in 1592 and became known as the Wine Well and a 'rarity most remarkable'. Its reputation grew and the local masons built Keith Lodge for the convenience of patrons who included General Wolfe who then devised the stratagem of enlisting Highlanders for his campaign in North America. The benefit to the Government would be two-fold. Abroad, their presence would give excellent service to the British Army. At home, their absence would remove a lot of troublesome opposition to Government. There were six springs by 1815 but as with other springs in Britain their popularity declined by the end of the century. In the eighteenth century Kinghorn became famous for a Spa Well, and its reputation lasted for nearly two centuries and laid the foundation of the town as a resort. Six popular wells were promoted: in Wick, St Fergus Well; in Wigtown, the White Pump Well (1742); in Strathaven, St Anne's and St. Tann's Wells; in Lauder, St Nathan's Well; and in Edinburgh, St Bernard's Well.

Several towns prospered from the reputation of the waters. Strathpeffer had wells which were being frequented by the end of the seventeenth century because of their reputed healing properties. In 1777 Colin Mackenzie, minister of the parish and factor of the Cromarty estates, wrote to the commissioners of the annexed estates proposing the building of a 'House, Kitchen and Stable' for the accommodation of visitors, most of whom came from Aberdeen and Sutherland. He emphasised the amenities of the area – romantic walks, good hunting, as well as the advantages to the local people who would have a market for their agricultural produce. The commissioners did nothing. About twenty years later Dr Morrison of Elrick, Aberdeenshire, visited the Strath seeking relief from arthritis. He was cured and decided to take up residence at the head of the Strath. Due to his efforts a timber pump room 40 feet (12.19 metres) long was built and a regular service established in 1819. In 1817 the pavilion, concert hall and gardens were added and walks and drives were laid out leading into the woods and hills. The Spa Hotel, where Kinellan Drive is now situated, was opened a few years later. In 1839 Mr Gordon, an Irish M.P., opened an institution for those of limited means, with accommodation for fifty patients, and in 1858 as a memorial to Dr Nicholson Mackenzie, nephew of a local minister, who perished at sea, his mother built a hospital for twenty arthritic patients, now a physiotherapeutic unit. The Hydropathic Hotel – as at Peebles, Crieff, Melrose and Dunblane – became an important element in the progress of holiday and health resorts during the nineteenth century.

Public wells

Wells for normal consumption of water became prominent in most towns probably from the point when water courses through the towns began to become polluted in medieval times. In some cases they probably remained plain, but more solid and ornamental examples still survive. They were positioned at convenient intervals along the High Streets or closes. Most wells latterly were probably operated by hand pumps. In addition to the public wells numerous private wells were sunk in yards and gardens from earlier times, and these are occasionally uncovered during excavations. With the building of reservoirs and the introduction of piped water about the middle of the century all these wells fell into disuse. Where several public wells served a town they were given names to distinguish them, as the Lion Well, Dog Well, Cross Well, St Michael's Well(**65**) and New Well – all at Linlithgow.

The overcrowding of towns

Corrupting decay was visited upon the cities and larger industrial towns as they filled up with destitute families from the countryside, first from the Lowlands, but mostly from the Highlands. Next, Irish immigrants arrived following crop failures and famine. They were strangers to urban living. They crowded into any place that gave them a roof. Families shared rooms and slept on the floors. In their crofts they may not have had sanitary facilities but there were a stable and byres. In the older town houses there were often also no privies: there was only the gutter and streets. Conditions led to illness, epidemics and high death rates, especially in Greenock, a port convenient to travellers from Ireland and the Highlands. By the middle of the nineteenth century over 9,000 people were packed into the mid-parish limited to only 40 acres (16.19 hectares) giving a density of 470 persons per acre (1,160 per hectare)(**66**). In 1877

65 Linlithgow: St Michael's Well. Public street wells were vital to burghs up to the nineteenth century, when piped water was introduced throughout Britain. Linlithgow possessed a series of wells along the length of the town furnished with hand pumps and designed in stone.

66 Greenock: 8 Manse Lane, 1931. The photograph includes thirty-six adults and children. The Garden City movement of the 1920s to 1940s prompted strong reaction against such compact housing in the land behind the main streets of towns. Legislation was passed to encourage comprehensive compulsory purchase by the authorities and the clearance and provision of housing on new sites beyond the centres.

the town was clearing out blocks in the slums where net densities had reached an average of 900 per acre (2,223 per hectare) with the highest densities at 1,600 persons per acre (3,950 per hectare). By that time ninety-three percent of the population was lodged in various sorts of accommodation which had no form of any kind of sanitary facilities attached. In Tillicoultry, by about

1840, one-quarter of the families were living at a density of seventeen persons per house, and the mortality rate exceeded that of any other town in Britain.

In Edinburgh the uncontrolled influx of families concentrated in the Old Town, where a hundred years earlier tenement flats had been large and roomy. The local newspapers then advertised houses for sale in the closes with three to eight or nine fire rooms, and ancillary rooms such as garrets, dark rooms (or rooms without fireplaces). In the nineteenth century these once desirable town flats were split up and invaded, severely overcrowding and overloading the old structures. In some cases top storeys had to be removed; in others, total collapse occurred. In the six floors above the shops in a typical tenement in the Canongate in 1865 there were twenty-nine families totalling 103 persons living in thirty-six rooms with no sinks or water closets. Some tenements had slightly better arrangements with from three to twelve shared sinks and one or more water closets. The shocking aspect of these records is that some of the most overcrowded tenements without any water supply were built during this period of over-crowding as financial investments. These problems in Victorian days were experienced over much of the country. Liverpool had the highest density of population of any large city. In London in 1862 the densities in districts such as Whitecross Street or St Andrews in Holborn were at or in excess of 400 persons per acre (980 per hectare) compared with the Tron district of Edinburgh, the most crowded, of 314 persons per acre (775 per hectare).

The ravages of ill-health in the overcrowded old towns could not be permitted to continue. Epidemics of cholera and fever were developing to serious proportions despite the dedicated work of medical and health officials and charity workers. In Greenock typhoid in 1864 caused the death of the Inspector of the Poor and five doctors attending the sick. People had to be retained in the cities and industrial towns, for their labour was an essential element in industrial enterprise. The cure was eventually understood, and the era of tenement building by merchant/builders for workmen and their families began. The form of town extension then introduced was probably closer to the Scottish outlook in urban living than has hitherto been appreciated.

The Scottish tenements
Tenement building made the largest contribution to housing working people in the cities and towns during the greater part of the nineteenth century. Most tenements were of four storeys and laid out along the main roads or in gridiron patterns. Some streets were made reasonably wide to accommodate the tall heights resulting from high ceilings.

Unfortunately builders in Glasgow, under pressure to produce ever more houses to meet the rapid population growth, were permitted from about 1840 to insert rows of flats in some of the back clothes-drying greens, so lowering standards of light, air and amenity. In these instances densities grew up to about 1,000 persons per acre (2,470 per hectare).

The tradition of living in flats goes back to late medieval times in Scotland, and in this respect conforms to urban housing in many of the great continental cities such as Paris. It has been shown how the restricted availability of land in the fortified towns of Europe compelled builders to place apartments on upper floors to satisfy the need of the increasing number of citizens. This theory may also be applied to Edinburgh, but flat-building was introduced to small towns in the eighteenth century where land shortage did not exist – for example at Inverary. Shortage of sites was not a factor in Edinburgh after the first New Town and its many extensions were in progress, or in Glasgow by the last century, but four-storey tenements were still built in a variety of standards.

The machinery of tenure embraced in the Scottish legal system removed not only the restrictions on multiple title of the land but also the prohibition from ownership of individual floors in a block of flats which acted against flatted building in English cities.

In Scotland, builders could make greater profit in flatted building and were doubtless influenced by this. But more important than all these factors is the long-standing custom of vertical building in Scotland which goes back to tower houses – which, in turn, could be seen as a reversion to the first century B.C. brochs of the northern isles. Living on separate floors in tall buildings has become as normal to Scots as living in cottages is to Englishmen. In the preface to *Multi-Storey Living 1974* it is stated that flats are usually associated with low standards of accommodation and 'undesirable socio-cultural phenomena'. The author accepts that this does not apply to Scotland, but goes on to observe in the sublime ignorance of a patriotic Englishman that in the question of flatted housing, as in so many other aspects Hibernian [*sic*] practice scarcely impinges on British [*sic*] customs and attitudes except as it reinforces them, revealing that his apparent ignorance of geography may not exceed his ignorance of history. It is plain, however, that tenants in English industrial towns were treated with contempt by some of their flat builders. As late as 1877, for example, Liverpool had three-storey and five-storey blocks of flats placed only 25 feet (7.62 metres) apart. In 1844 builders in Birkenhead built four-storey flats in seven rows with only about 18 feet (5.48 metres) between them. They cynically called them Dock cottages. Some flats in the cities measured only 10 feet 6 inches (3.2 metres) square. Bedrooms could be 9 feet 6 inches x 7 feet (2.89 x 2.13 metres) or as narrow as 6 feet (1.82 metres). The English authorities last century apparently were caught unprepared for flat building and did not seem to have adequate legislation to prevent such exploitation. It is no wonder that tenement living is viewed with prejudice in England. The greater experience and powers of the Dean of Guild Courts in Scotland prevented such excesses — apart from the overbuilding of the garden areas in some parts of Glasgow.

The miners' rows

The coal masters in the mining towns favoured single storey terraces of one room houses for the miners. In 1842 houses were confined within a square plan of 18 feet 6 inches (5.63 metres). The principal room measured 18×12 feet (5.63×3.65 metres), and the two ancillary closets were each 9×6 feet (2.74×1.83 metres). Some owners planned for more rooms, but even at the end of the century miners' rows were being built to similar standards and with minimum space between for roads and gardens. Coal houses and dry privies were positioned at the rear of the rows.

Parks and tree planting in towns

The Victorians excelled in the reservation of acres of park land in towns for the health and recreation of inhabitants; land was set aside for parks even though building promoters were greedy for land to build on. Sometimes benefactors purchased the land and donated it to the community, or a local landowner made the gift directly.

In the eighteenth century trees were often planted in avenues in towns. In Edinburgh, for example, Elm Row was a wide pleasance reserved for pedestrians so that the merchants and their ladies could enjoy a summer evening stroll. It is now one of the widest city streets in Britain, but the trees have gone, apart from some recent planting.

In the smaller towns, trees were introduced into the wider market streets — such as at Crail(18, p.41), Inverkeithing, Lochmaben and Dalkeith. But this enthusiasm did not last because in many cases as soon as the trees matured and began to make their presence felt, they were cut down. This destructive attitude has become one of the less attractive traits of Scottish towns. If a townsman is given a saw and immediately reacts by cutting down a tree, he will be a Scot. If he cuts down a street full of trees, he will also be a drainage or water engineer. For this reason the sight of the fine spreading trees so carefully preserved in English towns and villages is much rarer in Scotland and cannot be attributed merely to climate or Dutch Elm Disease. Over a decade ago many towns began again to plant trees in roads and gardens, and although vandals and some dry summers have led to losses, the improvement is being revealed yearly, and if the trees continue to escape the attentions of the man with the saw, they will bring delight to generations to come. Especially valuable are the attempts to reintroduce trees into the spaces at the backs of the buildings in the main streets of the medieval centres of towns. There they are seen to great effect because of the otherwise barren aspect such areas produce when covered only with paving and road surfacing. Trees also make the presence of commercial yards, car parks and storage areas more acceptable in appearance, particularly in areas which at the inception of the towns were intended for cultivation and tree planting as well as for use as yards and outhouses.

Churches

During the seventeenth century the burghs preserved their parish churches, notably at Haddington, Linlithgow, Stirling, Perth and Edinburgh. Fortunately the abbey churches were saved at Paisley and Dunfermline. Glasgow's great cathedral was spared along with Dunblane Cathedral and Brechin (partly demolished and rebuilt in 1806). Some of the collegiate churches may still be seen, sometimes the richest architectural parts in semi-ruins – for example, at Dunglass.

All the burghs had churches in medieval times, but a small number shared a church with others outside the burgh. Because of extreme puritanical beliefs in the later sixteenth century and the seventeenth century, only the plainest of churches were favoured. A jewel like Restalrig Church near Leith was condemned by stern prophets of the Kirk as a monument of idolatry to be raised and utterly cast down and destroyed. The baleful countenance which the puritans cast on Scotland's art and architecture in these times blighted the artistic soul of her people for centuries. During that time some surviving churches were abandoned to be replaced by new churches, so that the ruins of the older buildings still remain, as at Selkirk and Penicuik. The greatest impetus to church building was prompted partly by the growth of population in the large towns at the beginning of the nineteenth century, and later by the remarkable increase in nonconformist sects. Relief Churches and Churches of Ease had to be erected to accommodate new parishioners. From the middle of the eighteenth century the Scottish Episcopalian Church, the Church of Scotland and the Roman Catholic Church (representing the older establishments) found in their presence Jewish synagogues, Baptist churches, Methodists, Congregationalists, Glassites, Seceders, New Light and Old Light Burghers, the Free Church, the United Presbyterian Church, the Free Presbyterian Church, the United Free Church and the Unitarian Church. These bodies grew out of the highly-charged debates when fervent believers vehemently expatiated on such issues as Arianism, Erastianism, secession, disruption and antidisestablishmentarianism – which enriched both ecclesiastical experience and the English Dictionary(**67**). As if to atone for the previous generation's negative attitude towards church architecture, Victorian churchmen and architects dedicated their financial and artistic resources to produce the finest building their combined forces could muster. The best architects of their times were summoned, such as Playfair, Bryce, Skae, Gillespie-Graham, Pugin, Gilbert Scott, Burn, Pilkington, Slater, Milne, Starforth, Wilson, Brown, Thomson, Rowand Anderson, Mackintosh and many others. The exuberance of their conceptions found expression only after some of the Church bodies adopted a more tolerant position from the middle of the century onwards. Then stained glass was permitted in Glasgow Cathedral, and many an upright Church elder must have wondered who could have dared to bring painted glass into the House of the Lord. In the plans for new churches in the decades that followed, elevations and perspectives gave an impression of chaste, simple buildings, but in the making, ornamentation became more evident. For the Barclay Church in Edinburgh and South Church in Penicuik, Pilkington completed his works in a crescendo of rich stone carving and stained glass born out of his haunted imagination,

67 'The Disruption Worthies'. The caricaturist depicts several eminent churchmen whose names are commemorated in churches such as Candlish and Chalmers.

68 East Linton. A small burgh which gently rises to the top of a mound. It is built in grey and pink stone with slates and terracotta pantiles. The comely church amongst the low, leafy trees offers a welcoming completion at the head of the town.

69 Peebles: High Street. The late twelfth-century High Street is now lined with a variety of buildings in stone or black-and-white painted surfaces belonging to the last three centuries and representing styles such as Georgian, mock Tudor and Baronial. The parish church tower is balanced at the opposite end by a happy conjunction of roads generating many picturesque urban compositions.

even introducing symbolic doctrinal features which probably escaped the notice of his clients.

In this way Scottish towns acquired an astonishing collection of imaginative buildings probably unequalled in Europe. Their spires and towers contribute powerfully to the skyline, their typical modelled shapes give maximum interest to a street or square, and the details of carving and masonry are a constant delight. Vigilance must be kept among all this richness in order to prevent its being lost on account of its very profusion(**20**, p.43, **44, 68, 69, 70, 71**).

Monuments

Memorial statues to royalty, noblemen, military heroes and local worthies proliferated in the nineteenth century. Classically inspired equestrian statues and columns were especially admired. In Edinburgh, James Craig's proposal for an equestrian statue in each of the squares in his New Town Plan was only partly carried out: an equestrian statue of Prince Albert stands in Charlotte Square, but St Andrew Square has the 150 foot high (45.7 metres) stone column topped with a statue of Henry Dundas, 1st Viscount Melville(**70**). A twelve-ton statue of the Duke of Wellington on his prancing war horse stands outside Register House in Princes Street. Edinburgh has the oldest equestrian statue in Scotland, incidentally: the statue of Charles II in Parliament Square, dated 1685, is also the oldest statue in Edinburgh(**36**, p.80).

In the nineteenth century, other equestrian statues were erected in Glasgow and smaller towns such as Selkirk and Hawick, and columns were raised in Elgin(**21**, p.44), Glasgow and Coldstream(**15**, p.38). Statues were erected to kings(**72**), queens (notably Queen Victoria) and commoners(**20**, p.43). As time passed, some were pushed aside or removed in much the same way as market crosses and ports – because they had become obstacles to carriages, and later, cars. Most of the statues remain, however, to give historic and artistic enlightenment to townspeople – because Scots, unlike many nations, have not in their midst those who either pull down or blow up monuments.

Ornamentation of towns was frequently proposed but rejected in whole or part. The great scheme for a National Monument on Calton Hill(**73**) in Edinburgh began but was then halted in the 1820s, and was not restarted despite an appeal in 1907. Sir Frank Mears and Ramsay Traquair suggested adapting the scheme by discontinuing the colonnade, but infilling the sides with small scale separate monuments and buildings. It is possible that with modern materials the exterior could be replicated with glass-reinforced concrete columns and cornice to simulate the stone, and the interior finished like a modern framed building in steel and glass for an exhibition in acknowledgement of Scotland's great past and confidence in as great a future.

Mears proposed a Via Sacra in Johnston Terrace on the road up to Edinburgh Castle in a tribute to the Scottish Regiments of the First World War. Ports into the Old Town were proposed: one exciting example by Sir Patrick Geddes at the foot of Ramsay Lane, another by Sir Frank Mears at the Nether Bow as a monument to King Edward VII. A classical Triumphal Arch was designed earlier by Gillespie-Graham across the West End of Princes Street which would not only have commemorated Waterloo, but also restricted heavy traffic in the rest of the street (**74**).

70 Edinburgh: George
Street looking east.
Intended in the
eighteenth century as
the chief residential
address in the city,
George Street quickly
surrendered to
commercial interests.
The architecture
suffered as a result, but
the first detrimental
effect occurred earlier,
when the site of St
Andrew's Church was
moved from the end of
the vista to the site
illustrated. The
insurance building at
the south-east end of
the street was well
designed but dwarfs
the Melville Column in
rising too far above the
four-storey limit of
George Street. Finally,
St James's Centre
beyond St Andrew
Square violates the
conception of the
correct climax.

71 Elgin. The burgh
was fortunate in its
choice of architects for
its earliest buildings.
The classical church
rises to the occasion
with that
eighteenth-century
sense of perfection that
twentieth-century
architects should never
cease to study.

72 Edinburgh: George Street and George IV statue. The view westwards from the same point as plate **70** shows commercial intrusion accomplished with restraint.

73 Edinburgh: National Monument. Looking east from Princes Street, the picture shows two hundred years of the city's architectural history: the well mannered good taste of the eighteenth century almost eclipsed; the awe-inspiring power of Victorian grandeur; the 'land of hope and glory' architecture at the turn of the century; a touch of the chill, lonely post-war nudity; and in the background the as yet unfulfilled dream of the glory of ancient Greece.

In the late nineteenth century McCaig accomplished his memorable monument in Oban. In Edinburgh a Galashiels joiner named George Kemp gave Scotland the most original, dynamic and appropriately conceived romantic Gothic monument in Europe(**75**). With the forthcoming publication of a new edition of *The Works of Sir Walter Scott,* it is time for his monument to be refurbished and accorded the acclaim it deserves. George Kemp, as designer, might also be recognised properly by the posthumous award of Honorary Fellowship of

74 Edinburgh: design by Gillespie-Graham for a memorial to Waterloo in Princes Street, 1820. The plan comprised rooms on the upper floors to house the records of the battle, where thousands of Highlanders of all ranks distinguished themselves and played a major role in the victory.

the R.I.A.S. which would put an end to the custom of referring to him as a mere joiner.

The classical planners placed the monuments in squares and at the focus of a street. The Victorians liked to place them in settings of open gardens with benefit to monument and garden. Scott's monument placed in Princes Street Gardens conforms perfectly to a street that Victorian architects made their own.

Many towns after 1918 put up war memorials – from simple catafalques in the cities to fine bronze sculptures in the smaller communities. The National Shrine was executed in the Scottish style at Edinburgh Castle. Some towns, as in Victorian times, placed the monuments at the entrances to parks. Leith chose to make a practical gesture and collectively paid for the building of a children's wing to its hospital. It is a fundamental requirement that a monument should last. Hospitals do not last, especially when taken out of the hands of the community by boards and officials uninterested in commemorative intentions. So Leith could be the first town to have its memorial destroyed. Although Lewis Mumford in the 1930s acclaimed the death of the monument in America, sculpture and monuments continue to live in Scottish towns, and modern examples in recent years have been erected in Edinburgh, Dalkeith and elsewhere.

135

75 Edinburgh: Sir Walter Scott's Monument (late nineteenth-century view). Admired in the last century for its imaginative conception, the monument has been regarded with distaste by the twentieth century. Its recognition as a *tour de force* of Victorian design is long overdue.

Experiments in residential planning

Interesting experiments in Edinburgh in two-storey flats for artisans orginated from the ideas of a number of reformers, including A. MacGregor and Sir James Gowans at Gardeners Crescent. Other collaborators were the geologist and stonemason Hugh Miller and the Rev. Dr James Begg, a pioneer in housing improvement for working people. They founded the Co-operative Building Company and in 1861 started a scheme called 'The Colonies' at Stockbridge. The scheme produced three new ideas. First, it was built by members of the co-operative themselves. Secondly, the blocks lying parallel at less than fifty feet apart had no backs. The lower floors, consisting of flats, had windows on each side but entrance from one side only. The upper flats, some with attic accommodation, also had windows on either side, but the open staircases outside leading up to each pair of flats were on the other side from that which contained the entrances to the ground floor flats. Thirdly, the scheme achieved a high density and a full standard of cross-ventilation, unlike the equivalent back-to-back houses then being built in the north of England. The standard of masonry was naturally high, and later, sculptured stones were built into the walls and bow windows added to give comfort and style. A similar scheme followed at Abbeyhill. The style of planning spread elsewhere, such as Dundee and Dalkeith, the block at Dalkeith having internal stairs (now demolished).

8 Urban Ideas in the Nineteenth Century and Twentieth Century

Unfulfilled visions

Since early in the age of Scottish Planning men have been inspired to conjure up visions of towns, but their schemes have not always been realised. In the second phase of royal burgh building at the beginning of the thirteenth century there stood the royal burgh of Auldearn concurrently with burghs like Dumfries, Ayr, Inverness and Lanark. Yet it did not prosper and only survived as a village of about 700 (maximum population). Similarly, Fyvie and Urr burghs of barony were chartered in the mid-thirteenth century but remained small villages. Many of the later burghs of barony have not even survived in name and may not have developed beyond the ambitious notions of their would-be promoters. In the mid-sixteenth century Rattray in Aberdeenshire was made a royal burgh, but two centuries later it became derelict after a great storm destroyed its harbour.

Some towns developed and then declined to extinction. Roxburgh has been mentioned previously. The inhabitants of Kelso burgh transferred from the old site to rebuild alongside the abbey. In later times the bold proposal for a New Edinburgh by James VII did not have support. Less exalted but by no means insignificant personages had aspirations in town creation. Lord Macdonald engaged Gillespie-Graham in 1810 to plan a complete New Town at Kyleakin in Skye, but it was not built. It was conceived in the grand Georgian manner forming in plan a crescent shape of two-storey terraced houses round the line of the coast. The scheme was regimented in parallel lines of very long blocks, and two churches with spires were to give points of interest in the otherwise regular roof lines. It would be difficult to imagine any town less appropriate to the island, and the sight of identical two-storeyed terrace houses stretching in never ending line along the margin of the bay would have stunned perception.

The plan for Kyleakin suffered the conceptual defect apparent in most of the architectural schemes of the time: they were only concerned to fulfill the domestic needs of the inhabitants. No provision was made for work, commerce, shopping, marketing or industry – only churches were admitted. In Montrose in 1793 a Mr N. Ross, proprietor of the island at the south of the South Esk, promoted a very different plan.

The outline, conditioned by the shape of the island, was trapezoidal, and internally the corners of the outline were joined by crossroads 65 feet wide (19.8 metres) which met at a large square 330 feet wide (100 metres). The formal layout was asymmetrical with similarities to the earlier plan of Keith but with the large houses ranged round the perimeter of the two main crossroads and at the crescent. Sites on the lesser roads were reserved for the smaller houses of artisans. From the outset, sites were allocated not only for a church but also for a fire station, markets for meat, fish, meal and grain, ship-building slips, a slaughter house, reservoir, inn, coachyard, stables and cemetery. One of the two bridges was to be equipped with a lifting section to allow the passage of vessels of up to 500 tons. Elevations of the houses were to be provided by the proprietor, and stone and lime were available on the mainland. William Sibbald, Superintendent of Works in Edinburgh, was concerned in the production of the plan. This project did not proceed.

By the end of the eighteenth century it is evident that some proprietors and their planners understood there was more to a town than houses and a church. Yet for decades in Edinburgh, Glasgow and other parts, promoters and their architect-planners seemed determined to press on with their exclusively residential schemes which persistently proved to be inadequate in terms of burghculture.

At the turn of the eighteenth century the great activity in the north-east of Scotland resulted in the building of many new villages. Some landowners were not successful: Covesea, New Leeds and Tomintoul were only partly built, and at Slioch, Plewlands and Waulkmill the promotions were abandoned at the planning stage. Near Fochabers a second new village was projected which would join with its neighbour to achieve a large single town, but it was not begun. A new fishing town at Cullykham Bay in Banffshire was planned but not built. More than a dozen such abortive ventures occurred at that time.

A unique plan for a village at Dunninald in Angus was produced by John Playfair in 1780. Intended as a complete model village, the project was unfortunately terminated at the planning stage. Building started in 1827 on Robert Owen's design for a perfect town, Orbiston, but, as always, the ideal was beyond reach and no visible remains of his vision may be found on its site.

In August 1806 a topical proposal was submitted by an engineer to drive a twin tunnel under the Forth from South Queensferry to Rosyth. The site had been meticulously surveyed, the geological conditions established and the levels determined. Each tunnel was to be 15 feet (4.57 metres) in diameter with a 9-foot (2.74 metres) wide carriageway and 3-foot (0.91 metres) wide footpaths. Grieve, the engineer, estimated the cost at £164,000 and the projected time to completion as four and a half years. In the period after the Second World War another project was investigated for a tunnel or 'tube', but the road bridge was preferred.

The rejection of the far-seeing endeavours of Grieve is to be regretted. However, at the same time the Edinburgh citizens thwarted a proposal to build along the south side of Princes Street – proof that the community could recognise and halt an inept concept borne of the narrow vision of their civic leaders.

Since much of Scotland's intellectual talent was concentrated in Edinburgh in the early nineteenth century, ideas were forged and vigorously canvassed on how Edinburgh should be planned and built. In the struggles, architects criticised architects, speculators conspired and manoeuvred. The city shows the results of those who were victorious. Those who were vanquished have left only their plans and pleas.

In the 1780s Robert Adam threw his considerable resources into capturing the commission as architect for all the building works in the North Bridge of Edinburgh, including the University. James Craig also prepared plans for the area. The grandiose opulence of both schemes was more than the Town Council or anyone else could have financed.

Mr Trotter, his argument supported by Elliot's drawings, put forward in 1834 a classic plan for improving the Mound, which on sound planning grounds incorporated an arcade of shops serviced with central heating. Architects Hamilton, who had earlier submitted alternative proposals, and Burn, independently poured scorn on the scheme for reasons of town design and economics. It seems that their aesthetic arguments were probably dubious and their economics suspect. The Mound remained much as it is today, but with the National Gallery added later.

In the early 1820s a plan was made to introduce large villas into the land on the west of the New Town bordered by Ann Street and St Bernard's Crescent on the east, and Comely Bank on the north. A very low density of about one house to the acre was indicated, with sites varying from small to very large. Instead of the classical balanced approach, informality governed the lay-out. Straight streets mingled with winding streets. Broad avenues and geometrical crescents were reserved for the main routes. Most original was the forest of trees bordering all the boundaries of each plot so that the individual grounds whether large or small were treated like parks to mansion-houses. The lay-out was ahead of its time and foreshadowed the Garden City styles on a grander scale. No part of this romantic riposte to the classical architectural ideals of eighteenth-century Edinburgh was built. A density of about eight persons to the acre implied too big a loss of revenue from feuing for the speculators who, in the earlier New Town schemes to the east, had been working on as many as ninety persons to the acre.

A proposal similar in many features to the lay-out of the scheme near Comely Bank was made for land at Trinity to the

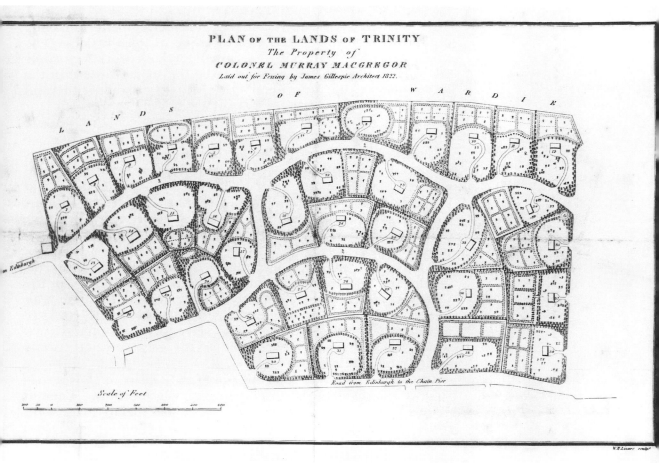

PLAN OF THE LANDS OF TRINITY
The Property of
COLONEL MURRAY MACGREGOR
Laid out for Feuing by James Gillespie Architect 1822.

76 Edinburgh: plan for feuing land at Trinity, by Gillespie-Graham, 1822. In terms of planning, the design was far ahead of its time, but a low economic return for the builders is the probable reason why it was not adopted.

west of Leith(**76**). Few straight lines were employed, other than at the perimeter of the land to be feued and at the divisions between plots. But the internal arrangement of planting showed that the planners had visualised each house to be placed near the centre of the plots of about four-fifths of an acre (0.32 hectares) and to be surrounded by a tree-lined park with curved boundaries and specimen trees distributed at selected points between. The plan was made in 1822 by the office of James Gillespie (later Gillespie-Graham). The curvilinear form of lay-out was in vogue at that time: for example, it was employed by Benjamin Ferry in the 1830s for his plan of early Bournemouth, introducing winding streets and much tree planting. Ferry was a friend of Pugin who worked with Gillespie-Graham much later on Tolbooth St John's Church in Edinburgh, but there was no direct connection through Pugin, who was a boy when the Trinity plan was conceived.

A network of winding roads is confusing to strangers, who can get lost in the maze and feel that they will need to navigate by the sun to escape. The lay-outs of the proposals for Comely Bank and Trinity were far removed from the traditional logical town plans for Scotland. The system was not merely pattern-making but an extreme resort to the picturesque in town-making. The traditional town plans were designed for busy working people going from one address to another by the shortest route in the least time. In the picturesque town, travel distance, time and directions are unimportant; there needs only to be time for leisure and the enjoyment of living and moving about in pleasing surroundings.

Elsewhere in Edinburgh, ideas submitted by four competitors in 1817 for the planning of the area between Leith Walk and Easter Road were not adopted. Two were rather stiff and probably falling out of fashion. The others suggested shorter, straight streets and more flowing lines. Aspects of the latter designs were adopted by Playfair in a plan he successfully proposed to the city council three years later. Playfair, however, did not follow Stark's penetrating evaluation of the site and its possibilities – probably because he was too attuned to the professional attitudes of architectural theory of his time. But when construction of his elegant plan was partially accomplished, it was tossed aside to make way for a railway yard which the council no doubt felt was of greater value to city business and the railway company.

In Glasgow, a nobly conceived plan at Gorbals for a Regency suburb was begun at the end of the eighteenth century. Then in 1800 a railway was cut across the area to take coal to an adjacent ironworks. It struck to the heart of the scheme like a dagger, and the plan collapsed. The few newly-built terraces were deserted and later occupied by overcrowded poor families living in houses intended for only one family each. The area declined rapidly well before the end of the nineteenth century, the splendid vision of Laurieston obliterated by one of the most disreputable slums in Europe.

In the mid-war years of this century a dramatic plan for the extension of Edinburgh University was produced by Sir Frank Mears. It made use of the ground to the east of the University which was generally occupied by buildings of lesser worth. A University Avenue was projected focussing on the McEwan Hall on the west, and a new building on the east lying below Salisbury Crags. This was a site and situation ready for architectural grand opera. From the foot of the slope at the east end the McEwan Hall and a new chapel and Union would rise impressively above – equal in drama to the view from the top towards the Crags. A secondary avenue to the north was focussed on the old quad and the dome. The scheme was rejected by the authorities, who at the time thought there was no evidence to suggest that so large a scheme would be required. Although the Clyde Report on 'City Development – 1943' recommended that the University should expand to the east, the University commissioned a plan to redevelop the ground to the south of the University. The plan required the demolition of George Square — in which, it was conceded, there were certain buildings of architectural merit but not of first-class order. The earlier plan of Sir Frank Mears was criticised because it was then sixteen years old and had not allowed for expansion of proposed buildings, but the University did not give Mears an opportunity to revise his plan or show its capabilities for expansion. The University claimed that its plan was noble and inspiring.

Forty years later, the results are on site for the study and enlightenment of all who are interested in the planning of a town and its architecture. The redevelopment of the south-side and the demolition of George Square provide us with an opportunity to judge whether, in the University's words, 'a work of genius [has been] evoked in which the City of Edinburgh and Scotland will feel a lasting pride'.

The post-war years thrust planners upon Scottish town councils who should have known better than to permit their fantasies to be published. Abercrombie's plan for Edinburgh was so absurdly unachievable as to suggest that he probably did not know himself what he was up to. The plan for Glasgow sought to superimpose over the central area a traffic complex to give every Glasgow motorist the thrill of a lifetime, and all the residents a hell of a lifetime. In both cities calamity was easily averted by doing very little or nothing about it and adhering to the fact that what may have been a bright vision to one person could be a nightmare for others.

The Garden City movement in Scotland

From the period after Sir Christopher Wren up to the end of the nineteenth century, new styles in architecture in England had nearly always been initiated by Scottish, or Anglo-Scottish architects — like Chambers, Gibbs, the Adam brothers, Campbell, Stuart, 'Capability' Brown, Shaw and Tite. Then in 1898 an Englishman and great humanitarian, Ebenezer Howard, published *To-morrow*, revealing his idyllic utopia. Its theme was imaginative and apparently practical. Towns could be made with houses and gardens at about ten houses to the acre (27 per hectare), and be furnished with industries and social requisites for everyone.

The message reached and convinced all kinds of people. Its influence came to work in the new towns in England — at Port Sunlight, Letchworth and Welwyn, in the suburbs of Wythenshawe in Manchester, at Becontree, and at estates in Hayes and Acton. The notion of Garden Cities spread abroad to the continent of Europe, and especially to North America, where Greenbelt was built at Maryland in the mid-1930s, and in the 1960s, Reston and Columbia were begun.

In Scotland, Howard's work affected planners such as Sir Patrick Geddes and Sir Frank Mears. Howard visited Greenock to give advice on planning a Garden City there, but unfortunately he seems to have been unwilling to acknowledge some insurmountable obstacles to his proposals which the difficulties in the terrain presented.

The examples in England of the Garden City theory were admired by visiting Scottish councillors and others. The schemes gave evidence that when correct techniques were adopted and planners and architects such as Raymond Unwin, Barry Parker and Alwyn Lloyd employed, the results could be most attractive – embodying all the charm and sweetness of English domestic building in perfect surroundings. It is therefore disappointing to look upon the attempt to transplant the style into Scotland and realise how in the building it failed to blossom. There were factors at the outset unfavourable to success. The English architects and planners achieved a harmonious relationship of scale between houses, roads and spaces. The heights of the two-storey cottages were restricted by low ceilings, by using only one or two steps up to the ground floor, by dropping the eaves at places below the full heights, and at times incorporating dormer windows. The road widths were often narrower than the Scottish standard of 20 feet (6.09 metres), and in short roads, pavements were merely refuges of about 2 feet (0.6 metres).

By comparison, Scottish houses were taller by about 2–3 feet (0.76–0.91 metres). Scottish builders also favoured flatted two-storey blocks of four houses. These were broader than cottages and therefore bulkier and with larger roofs. Pavement widths were never less than 5 feet (1.52 metres). English building was executed in the traditional facing brick or was whitewashed, but the Scottish houses were seldom faced with traditional stone. Very significantly, the promoters of Scottish examples failed to understand that a Garden City was an amalgam of buildings and gardens. To be successful, the nature of the plans required well designed gardens as well as sympathetically designed houses and buildings. Scottish sites probably started at a disadvantage because the farming and field system from which building sites were enclosed did not contain many tree-lined lanes and field divisions. Even where some planting did occur, authorities, professionals and builders conspired to fell the trees before building. Where trees were conserved, householders later exhorted authorities to remove them. Lastly, in areas less favoured climatically, garden plants do not grow as lushly as in the warmer counties in England.

The most successful Scottish examples of the Garden City were produced by the Local Government Board for Scotland in the west of the country and by the architect John A. W. Grant.

77 Galashiels: Lucy Sanderson Homes. An example of Scottish planning and domestic building in the manner of the best architects practising at the beginning of the twentieth century.

The Lucy Sanderson Homes at Galashiels by Mears and Carus-Wilson are the best Scottish interpretation of the style(**77**).

After 1918 the Local Government Board for Scotland was instrumental in having type plans for houses prepared under the Housing of the Working Classes Acts (1890–1909), a procedure which resulted in some good designs being adopted in the early post-war years. Admiralty housing was planned and designed at Gourock, Cambuslang and Glengarnock. The houses contained Scottish elements but were obviously influenced not undesirably by English design. The architects adhered to the technique of permitting the contours to guide the lines of the roads and the buildings. Terrace blocks were restricted to not more than eight houses in a row, and semi-detached blocks predominated. The Board recommended the retention of the natural amenities on a site as well as the 'judicious planting of trees and shrubs'. It was thought that the sub-division of the front gardens should be avoided and methods used to relieve the monotony of a long straight building line. The ceiling heights were 8 feet 6 inches (2.58 metres), and the ground floors were a minimum of 15 inches (381 mm) above the ground. It appears that at the outset of the post-1918 house building, sound advice on site planning was not lacking, but too many did not heed it.

The inadequacies of the between-wars housing areas have been recognised by those authorities who, since the 1960s, have planted trees and coloured the less pleasant roughcast walls of older housing schemes. The success of such improvements still leaves doubts about the wisdom of attempting to introduce into Scotland a form of planning and building attuned to the traditions and spirit of another country. It is odd that logical Scots did not apprehend that the more appropriate a solution is for the character of one country's towns and buildings, the less fitting it is likely to be for the character of another's.

Public buildings and commercial streets in late Victorian times and the twentieth century

Urban evolution did not cease in the Victorian age. There was the withering of the older parts, the burgeoning of the newer. The results of the emerging institutions and the changes in social attitudes became woven into the urban fabric and still survive.

As has been shown, Victorians valued city parks, so Scottish cities and towns now possess large parks with mature trees relieving the high-density areas of building. Some of these parks were created by benefactors – as in Edinburgh, where Thomas Hope had leased the Meadows in 1722 and by drainage and planting preserved a small part of the Burgh Muir. Later, Bruntsfield Links were also preserved. Victorian parks were laid out in many towns despite determined efforts by promoters to feu them as building lots. Victoria Park in Leith was confidently planned for house building in 1869, as had been Princes Street Gardens earlier in the century, but both these efforts were foiled. Urban open spaces were saved from development in many other towns, or were established during the late Victorian periods – as in Aberdeen, Elgin, Forfar, Dunfermline, Dalkeith, Lanark and Hawick.

Public buildings raised the dignity of town and city streets in the late nineteenth century. Halls, theatres, libraries, government offices, museums, galleries, headquarters of professional bodies and sheriff court houses occupied street sites alongside banks, insurance buildings, hotels and town churches (**71**, p.133, **78**). Hardly any of the buildings of that time failed to impress; many are of excellent design and few give offence. It was a period of freedom unabused. Architects and the public came to a reasonable consensus of what was liked.

In the classical period many burghs built towers and steeples – as at Banff, Newburgh and Auchtermuchty(**79**, **80**, **81**). During the late nineteenth century burghs built their new town chambers usually to Scottish Baronial designs(**82**). New banks adopted less romantic styles; schools and hospitals were plainer, except for some elaborate edifices. There are instances of larger buildings occupying sites surrounded by grounds, following the example of the forerunner of Heriot's Hospital in Edinburgh.

In the commercial streets round the turn of the century offices and shops appeared in the resplendent confident form of the 'land of hope and glory' style(**73**, p.134). All were built in stone worked by the best craftsmen. Thereafter, a Scottish tradition that had seemed everlasting and to date back for centuries was rapidly brought to a halt. It was as if stone quarries had suddenly all ceased to exist. Eminent architects also lost their

78 Kelso: the Square. The well preserved and carefully tended centre of Kelso, showing its classical civilised architecture.

sense of scale and architectural propriety: even stepping up to kick down sound stone architecture and replace it with 'slabricated' structures of concrete, aluminium, glass, and – heaven help Scotland – brick. These erections elbowed their way into the midst of streets in towns and cities with the same odious effect that a scruffily-dressed individual in jeans and no tie would make if he planted himself down beside his hostess at a Royal Banquet. Fortunately, most of the smaller burghs escaped the worst excesses of architectural misbehaviour and the new generation of architects is learning how to perform better and in more appropriate fashion.

Victorian villas

Although Gillespie-Graham's layout for villas in Trinity did not materialise on site, the public demand for suburban villa houses in gardens increased during the nineteenth century, and there are few towns which do not now possess areas consisting of gardens and trees with handsome ten-roomed stone houses with

79 Banff: Low Street. A good grouping of buildings at the centre rises from the stone-arched screen, the market cross and classical buildings, helped by the Adam steeple. The elements need to be clearly visible – a situation difficult to achieve because of street furniture and cars.

slated roofs and well designed interiors. This style of building continued into the first decade of this century and engaged the talents of most of the better architects. Many have been skilfully flatted to suit modern living. Others have been destroyed to make way for modern flats – including, unfortunately, the irreplaceable 'Rockville', Gowan's house in Edinburgh.

The bungalows of the 1930s

One of the unsatisfying products of the Garden City approach in Scotland was the mass building of bungalows. In the 1930s these were frequently referred to by critics as 'bungaloid growths'. A thousand would be set down in lengths of fifty of similar design

80 Newburgh, Fife. In the mid-eighteenth century the town replaced its ancient single-storey thatched houses with two-storey stone and slate cottages. The Fife-type town steeple was erected in 1802. The town now mixes seventeenth-century and eighteenth-century small scale Scottish styles with fine, balanced, larger houses of the same period. Painted fronts brighten the narrower section of the street.

81 Auchtermuchty: the Cross. The settlement was very early but did not become a royal burgh until the sixteenth century. Because it was not planned as a royal burgh it has an irregular layout, and the resulting charm is evident. Combining well are the Fife-style crow-stepped gables, the steep roofs and the tower and steeple – all at rest in classical repose, contrasting with the restless movement of the curving plan.

82 Forres. The tower and market cross possibly stand on the sites of the originals of 850 years ago. Their Victorian styles establish the unmistakable character of the town; their solidity should deter motorists from trying to remove them.

on either side of the straight roads outside a city, with no space in the small front gardens for trees or significant planting. The effect is not as daunting as the long nineteenth-century terraces in Lancashire mill towns and in some London suburbs, but the unrelieved monotony is more than was necessary. Some relief might have been achieved by compartmenting the larger streets into short lengths of about six units using hedges and house paint: on either side of the streets, hedges about 7 feet (2.1 metres) high could be planted across the front gardens between pavements and house frontages, and the house walls in each compartment could be painted in one distinctive colour. The fundamental error in the lay-out is that usually, many streets were too straight and long. The Scottish builders did not understand the need for the roads to be in scale with the bungalows, which are of small hamlet scale and not suited to long suburban roads.

There are critics of architecture and critics of architects. The former are fewer and are too seldom heard. The latter, being less informed and too vociferous, may wish to jump in among the 1930s bungalows and gleefully seize the opportunity to slander architects and town planners. Most of these schemes, however, were built without the benefit of the professionals. One merchant builder who assumed a gubernatorial posture in the industry defended their schemes as a complete success because they were in demand. It was a revelation to architects and others to listen to the salesmen's enthusiastic praise of their little houses with cream-coloured rooms, shiny apple-green doors and windows, and midget kitchenettes. Even more amazing was the rapturous admiration of the ladies as they toured their dream houses and promptly handed over the £500 price (£75 extra for a garage). The houses sold like hot cakes – over 100 in one day, and after all these years, they are still sought. At the time, Prime Ministers, Cabinet Ministers, Politicians, Lord Provosts, Treasury Officials, City Treasurers, economists, shop-keepers and the newspaper-vendor at the corner praised the bungalows. Their popularity demonstrates that in the matter of urbanculture, public taste does not invalidate judicious criticism. Today, the combined strengths of the Planning Acts, official and voluntary amenity bodies and architects and planners usually help to ensure successful results when burgh extensions and adaptations are proposed.

Twentieth-century New Towns

In the 1930s a proposal was made for a New Town scheme at Newbattle in Midlothian. It was based on the policy of Sir Frank Mears to plan and control growth of population in the countryside by linking villages and towns. The Newbattle plan was commendable. It proposed to join Dalkeith with Easthouses, Newtongrange and Bonnyrigg by creating a circular route round the abbey policies and infilling the areas on the perimeter between the existing communities with new houses, and it included a larger planned industrial estate to the south and another possible one to the west between Bonnyrigg and Dalkeith. The open centre, with its abbey policies, plantations, river and golf course, would have become the recreational and educational heart of this new combined community, which was described as a Ring Town many years ahead of Runcorn's ring plan. Unfortunately the idea was not developed after the war because of administrative problems and inadequate legislation.

Between 1947 and 1968 five New Towns were established: East Kilbride, Glenrothes, Cumbernauld, Livingston and Irvine. As yet these towns are without a history. So far, their characters only reveal the professional urban doctrine of their designers. None of the towns has yet achieved any sympathy with the characteristic life of the place it was established in. This lack of sympathy may be the indefinable missing quality which disturbs those who have moved to the New Towns from old, long-established communities. Like vintage wine, towns need time to mature before they can attain distinction. They can become more settled as a result of gradual change, turns of fashion and the ageing of the structures.

Like traditional towns, each of the New Towns has shopping and business centres and residential areas. In East Kilbride and Glenrothes, Garden City principles were adopted to give low densities of about twelve houses to the acre (29 per hectare). In the later towns, Cumbernauld, Livingston and Irvine, the densities were increased in accordance with the central government policy to conserve agricultural land which was applied to most large house-building schemes from the late 1950s up to the early 1970s. Local authorities and their architects were given no choice about building low-rise or high-rise flats.

The residential areas in all the New Towns are very similar to each other, and local character or recognisable individual themes are not very evident. If a theoretical town planner were to attempt to define these residential areas, using typical jargon, he might describe them as 'out-of-town suburban living complexes'. Many sections however, especially those more recently planned, do have pleasing aspects which will improve as the landscaping matures and more trees are planted, and as the walls and roofs mellow in colour.

The character of the older towns resides largely at the historic centres. More thought on the part of the designers of New Towns could have given the centres both a local character and a Scottish flavour – especially if the designers had followed in modern terms the urban qualities of the traditional examples. Plans based on wide, tapering, curving open High Streets, or triangular market-places, or double-curved rectangles (as in medieval Dundee) or on other such forms, would have given a ground plan round which a centre could develop. The space could be paved, planted with trees and flowers, adorned with sculpture, dominated by a twentieth-century market cross or symbol and furnished with seats, poster and exhibition stands, areas for outdoor events by dancers, or instrumentalists, or space for the Christmas tree – in short, a centre to suit all. Buildings placed along the edge of the space would incorporate shops, supermarkets, stores, banks, building society offices, travel agents, studios, restaurants, clinics and everything needed for a well provided centre. The upper floors would contain flats, commercial accommodation and offices. Churches, halls and hotels would be adjacent. Canopies, or the equivalent of the arcades of old Edinburgh, Linlithgow and Elgin, would line the frontages of shops to give shelter during inclement weather, and infra-red heaters fixed below the canopies would afford warmth in winter.

Apart from requirements governing the heights of frontage buildings (three, four or five storeys) and the nature and colour of materials, the proprietors and the architects of the New Towns would have been given freedom from the interference of planners to produce both plain but honest buildings and buildings of admirable architectural design. Such a policy would have encouraged genuine modern Scottish character in a fashion that would have helped to alleviate the sense of the missing human factor – the factor which history and native Scottish flair have given to the traditional centres. Relaxation in detailed planning control of building design enables the expression of the human factor – as exemplified in the streets of the towns in the north-east when Keith and Fochabers were built in the eighteenth century. Citizens living in the new planned towns of the twentieth century might agree that there can be too much planning.

Cumbernauld centre contrasts with traditional town centre planning. The centre has been described with approval as 'one of the most spectacular features of the town', 'rising grey like a dreadnought on the hilltop'. This no doubt honest description of a town centre built in neutral grey – a colour untypical of stone-built Scotland and giving an impression of a massive artefact of war – would not likely appeal to Scottish people. In England, Sir Frederick Gibberd produced his plan for Harlow only after a long and meticulous survey on site, searching out the details of planting, tracks, lanes, walls and other features of the site introduced naturally by years of occupation and husbandry. He studied the influence lines just as Scottish medieval planners had done, and he produced a town fittingly influenced by the landscape. In America, R. E. Smith made the picturesque modern Reston by respecting the established landscape, and the designers of Columbia achieved an equally impressive town, although they introduced a spectacular lake at the centre. Unfortunately, the enlightened understanding of town making which inspired these examples shone less brightly on those who built the modern New Towns in Scotland.

Residential planning and social disharmonies

There is growing evidence that those concerned with social behaviour or with maintenance of law and order will, in the near future, call for protective measures to be taken in the planning of new residential areas. The bleak vision is of houses or flats with a front door leading along a fenced path to a pavement on a busy road. All open spaces would be put behind fences with a few gates which would be locked at night. Gone would be the quiet, pleasant path sheltered from road noise. Walls not protected by unclimbable fencing would be faced with indestructible materials from which graffiti could be easily removed. Accessible house windows on the ground floors would be fitted with steel shutters or bars. Lockable compounds would enclose car parks. Tree-planting would be confined to a few areas permanently surrounded by security fencing. All areas open to the public would be covered with tarmacadam, not cobbles, setts or paving flags, as these are too easily removed to provide missiles. The Garden City movement would be superseded by the Fortified City movement.

These measures would attempt to alleviate the four problems which plague some residential areas: minor vandalism against property and planting, and graffiti-spraying; robbery and assault; car theft; and burglary. In the average residential area the miscreants and criminals represent a very small percentage creating fear and havoc in the rest of the community. The cost of protection would be high, and the effectiveness not total because the resourceful minds of ill-behaved children and hardened criminals are not easily thwarted.

Misbehaviour and law breaking have been a problem in towns since earliest recorded history. In early Scottish towns the mischievous child was punished by the parent or schoolmaster, adults could be put in the branks, branded on the face, nailed by the ear to the Tron, banished for all time from the towns, or hanged. The authorities did not much resort to fines or gaol sentences. Exhibiting the offenders and occasional branding advertised the convicted persons so that the well-behaved would recognise them in future.

Modern techniques of dealing with crime and misbehaviour have to be more delicately contrived. Sociologists may have to accept that the best way to achieve social peace is to acknowledge that in cities, like should live beside like. For harmony in any community it is essential that the residents share a common outlook on social standards of behaviour. People who are reasonably educated and have a regard for cleanliness and strict observance of conventional neighbourly behaviour will be alarmed if a newcomer arrives in their midst who cares little for their standards. It is not so readily admitted that people who put no value on cleanliness and accept untidy surroundings, noisy neighbours, and even petty thieving and occasional brawls, will resent people with different standards who live in their midst. If people wish to live a feckless existence, perhaps they are right to feel they should be left in peace to follow their own desires and instincts. If this unconventional minority were to be offered a low-rent, attractive housing scheme with simple unadorned houses and no trivial objects such as trees or screen walls, their acceptance would provide an economic, practical and positive solution to a serious social problem.

In modern times non-conformists in California, Europe and elsehwere choose to live in camps, patching up their shacks, making simple meals, wearing unconventional clothes in winter and none at all in summer, and seem happy and content. There should be no compulsion or coercion in these matters. If those who reject urban life realised that authorities are prepared to make separate areas of houses available for people of similar persuasion, and at minimal rents, such an experiment in a variant of urban living might meet the needs of a section of the community who are not well served by a system devised for those with different outlooks.

Residents would be free to come to the area or leave whenever they liked. The form of living they chose to adopt would be a matter only for themselves, and they would not have to submit to external interference over their style of life provided it did not interfere with the reasonable rights of others outside the group. Social care would ensure that people would not be obliged to live in an urban free-style area only because of economic difficulties.

If the experiment proved successful, other groups in residential areas could have the right to declare their area a high amenity area, or a noise protection zone, and so on. A constituted group would be licensed to manage land and streets, noise levels, regulations governing such matters as exercising dogs, play spaces for different age groups of children, parking areas, street colour treatment, garden maintenance and so on. Groups would be left to create their own standards of environment.

These innovations would not prevent crime and would not be intended to because crime emanates from a malfunction of the mind and spirit and not from the external influence of buildings, streets and gardens. Residents in towns would appreciate their being given the opportunity of living beside acceptable neighbours and in the knowledge that there was a wide choice of places in a town or city to permit everyone to practise their own ways of living.

Ultimately such district groups would send their own representatives to sit on the local council. Representatives would be elected on the strength of their public spirit and not national party politics – which have little relevance to the needs of urban life and may hinder rather than help them.

The distribution of industry from the turn of the eighteenth century to the twentieth century and modern centralised control

An attractive aspect of the early progress of industry in Scotland at the turn of the eighteenth century was the wide geographical spread. Wool, cotton and linen mills were built from Helmsdale in the north to Newton Stewart in the south. Landowners with sites and rivers to provide water power welcomed textile mills for economic reasons. By about the end of the eighteenth century textiles became Scotland's largest export. The wide distribution of economic advantages over the country was not impeded then by the strength of the great centres of industry in Glasgow and the south-west. During the later phase of the Industrial Revolution in the nineteenth century, the north of Scotland could not participate significantly because the principal elements, coal and iron, were located almost entirely in the south. The nature of these basic industries and the heavy industries which derived from them during the nineteenth century remained Scottish. It is only in recent years that Scotland's industry and employment have been brought within the influence of the powerful business interests in London, Tokyo and New York. It is difficult to see how such a growing concentration of power, if left uncontrolled, will not draw the substance and strength from weaker areas with the astronomical force of economic Black Holes.

It is obvious that the tradition of planning towns has now been stultified by current financial practices and the national crisis of debilitating doubt. The optimistic post-war plan created ideas and bold thinking in preparation for a new age of Scottish planning. New life was to be brought to old centres. The planning of new towns and suburbs was to be guided by sound Scottish traditions. These admirable resolutoins came to nought. Planning legislation leant heavily toward preventative urban therapy and tended to disregard the vital genetic factor in town evolution. The present planning generation now meekly accepts that positive planning in towns for a prosperous future is futile because the towns will not be allowed to have any future. But an attempt to hold the process of urban evolution at bay would be absurd. Arrested progression only admits active regression. New building in Scottish towns is being steadily reduced. Industries die or are removed. Projects to bring back new life to the communities are discarded. When in the near future the mis-shapen framework of the country's body-politic has had the necessary orthopaedic attention, towns will need to be ready for the consequences. Planners should not allow their gaze to be fixed on Georgian door knobs but lift their eyes to the challenging prospects on the horizon – and, if they have learned from Sir Patrick Geddes, even beyond.

9 Aspects of Modern Town Development

The story of Scotland's towns might be incomplete without an appraisal of current conditions and future trends. To do justice to such a theme would call for a more detailed account than can be given in a last chapter. That task must await another time. But a general survey of the principal topics of urbanculture today may alert us to the possibilities for improvement and help to prevent further deterioration.

Preserving local character

Scottish towns illustrate both good and bad practice in modern urbanculture. As the pace of change has increased in recent times, the centres of some towns have adapted well; others have suffered. In its manner of joining the past to the present each town exhibits distinctive qualities peculiar to itself. One test of sound practice in how best to join past and present is to examine the degree to which changes in towns have contributed to the maintenance of their character or to the revival of character in new forms.

One could cite ten examples representative of towns which have succeeded in this respect: Berwick – a Scottish town in England(8, p.21); Wigtown(**XIV**, p.57); Kelso(78, p.147); Peebles(69, p.131); Haddington(10, p.25, **VII**, p.31); Pittenweem(83); St Andrews(11, p.25); Arbroath(84); Melrose (85); and Elgin(71, p.133). These towns stand gracefully on their sites; the centres have handsome, well-formed plans; the buildings correspond with each other because their frontage widths are similar in length and their heights conform closely but not exactly. The materials and finishes harmonise in colour and texture and the styles of architecture of the buildings relate to each other. None of these towns represents perfection, for towns are a reflection of their inhabitants, but they have managed to preserve their individualities whilst accommodating change.

Local character – that 'historic filiation' which Geddes said derived from 'active sympathy with the essential and characteristic life of the plan concerned' – has been scorned by some professionals and entrepreneurs. The history of Dundee High Street is a sad example of such scorn.

Early in the nineteenth century Dundee High Street surpassed every street in Britain on account of its perfectly-placed buildings of excellent design united with an inspired medieval plan(**XII**, p.53). *Building Scotland* (1944) contains a picture of

83 Pittenweem. This is eighteenth-century harbour-side building in the finest Fife tradition.

High Street in 1885, by which time one of its fine buildings had been removed. It still retained its quality, however, compared with the 1935 photograph shown alongside. The intention of the authors was to demonstrate the amount of civic deterioration that can take place over fifty years. Nevertheless, the 1935 High Street still managed to retain its shape and scale. But thirty years later, most of the buildings had vanished. New building ignored every requirement of character conservation. The curving building lines, the basic unit lengths of building frontages, the established heights of building, the characteristic materials, the relationship of scale to the medieval tower, the essence of local architectural style – all these were sacrificed in the interest of financial success.

Other examples might be cited. In Leith, Kirkgate was one of the oldest streets in the country reasonably well preserved and rich in character. After years of municipal neglect it was uprooted in the 1950s and planted with meaningless rows of modern housing complete with a high-rise block. In Linlithgow, part of the High Street was rebuilt with modern white flats at a time when even the most illustrious of Scottish architects subscribed to the theory that the only way to rebuild in historic streets was to ignore all the lessons they taught. In Inverness, a town once graciously laid down beside the River Ness, the noble river front was roughly pushed aside by one of the worst groups of lumpish buildings to be found in Scotland(**86**). None of these misfortunes should have happened. Centuries of Scottish burgh planning provided the model, but it was not followed, nor were the advice and example of Sir Patrick Geddes.

The difficulties which confronted Dundee, Leith, Linlithgow and Inverness arose both from changes in modern urban living and the speed of change. The Dundee solution is change by revolution. The order of the day is to break with tradition, use municipal power to remove impeding building, and to fill up the new spaces with the over-large, cheap building designed by development companies for large retail operators, offices and others – most of whom have no connection with the town

84 Arbroath: High Street. Formerly congested with traffic, this is now a bright and busy but peaceful shopping street, thanks to the wisdom of the town council.

85 Melrose: Market Square. A well formed market-place badly obscured by motor traffic and directional signposts and bollards.

86 Inverness. When new building on one bank of a river in full view of the opposite bank is contemplated, the layout should be treated as a complete spectacle. This obvious approach to an urban problem was omitted in Inverness. The result is a collection of over-large constructions mechanically conceived, with the end seemingly inspired by a liquorice allsort.

concerned. The alternative is to provide for such new retail and office accommodation by adaptation, and to use techniques of town planning that do not conflict with character.

The problem of how modern towns should incorporate change involves a number of factors: motor traffic and pedestrians; architecture and conservation; business and commercial activities demanding large-scale premises; general amenity and the role of planners and town planning legislation. These five factors in modern town development have been changing towns, and their implications for the future of Scotland's towns can be judged by the changes already effected.

Motor traffic and pedestrians
Road traffic in town centres has created conflicts which could persist as long as motor vehicles survive. Most burghs try to

subdue these conflicts by traffic management, keeping the vehicles moving and carving out every small space to accommodate parked vehicles. The weakness of this policy can be seen on busy days when private and commercial vehicles are negotiating traffic systems, or trying to park, while pedestrians stand at the roadsides, either resigned to a delayed crossing or submitting to the indignity and danger of scampering across at the occasional gap in traffic.

This situation has been alleviated in some towns by the introduction of relief roads which divert a proportion of traffic out of the centre. With or without a relief road, the character of a town centre is impaired by the disturbance of traffic, and views of the town are obscured by the vehicles. If centres were cleared of traffic all the associated impedimenta could go with it: traffic signs; mini-roundabouts; bollards; and yellow lines – the worst blemish ever visited on busy Scottish towns. Proper paving to the roads could return, and trees and planting could reappear. Peaceful traffic-free centres would restore some civilised dignity to shopping and business and recreate spaces for people to linger or rest on benches.

Some towns have made a brave attempt. Arbroath paved a substantial part of its main shopping street and provided facilities for premises to be served at the rear for the delivery and despatch of goods(**84**). It has even succeeded in accommodating a large supermarket which has a street-entrance attractive in scale and character and large self-service premises at the rear. The shoppers' cars are also provided for at the backs of streets with ways-through. To date, Arbroath has yet to attend properly to these car parks, which need to be made tidy and have well-designed paving, planting of trees and flowers and some of the uglier back premises screened with hedges or walls. Authorities of ancient burghs who proceed with such schemes, incidentally, should ensure that expert archaeological advice is sought before excavations are permitted, otherwise the evidence of the building and the life of a burgh's people back to medieval times might be destroyed.

The burgh of Irvine adopted a most interesting approach to freeing the main shopping street for pedestrians. Decorative paving appropriate to the south-west of Scotland is brightly coloured. Up-to-date shop fronts have been fitted into the older buildings so that the best of old and new share the benefits of the original plan. A visitor to Irvine may not be able to avoid a view of a modern centre. This needed a large site, so the planners set it down astride the pleasant river and achieved the biggest planning flop in Scotland's history since the Commander of Antoninus Pius tried to prevent the two halves of the country from meeting by building a wall. It is conceded that Lollius Urbicus might have defended his project on the grounds that it was at least well sited, but this could not be said about Irvine's twentieth-century mistake.

Dingwall approaches the time when it too will have a fully functioning pedestrian centre with a display of pleasing buildings which merit greater recognition(**39**, p.83). Shopping areas in Glasgow and Edinburgh appear gradually to be turning more attention to the need for disentangling vehicular traffic and pedestrian activity to the benefit of all concerned. With skilled town planning many other burghs could improve their own shopping centres – for example, Dumfries and Perth (plans are in preparation), Cupar, Dalkeith, Dunfermline, Elgin, Forres, Haddington, Lanark, Montrose and Peebles. Logically planned towns such as these present less stubborn problems than do the anfractuous frameworks on which some English and Welsh towns have evolved – Birmingham, Durham, Macclesfield, Merthyr Tydfil, Norwich and Wolverhampton. Even London has directional problems of road layout, and Dublin in the nineteenth century developed a plan of unbelievable contortions compared with the cities of Edinburgh and Glasgow.

Where burghs are not yet able to find a workable solution to the traffic and pedestrian conflict only a slight shift of emphasis might be worthwhile. At the centre of Melrose the fine, curving triangular space, Market Place, contains the market cross in the middle and, on the perimeters, a range of Georgian and Victorian stone and painted buildings with roofs of slates from a variety of quarries(**85**). At the top of the centre glimpses are afforded of the landscape beyond. Urban character abounds but traffic does not because the roads meeting at the top of Market Place are a minor 'A' class road and two 'B' class roads. Unfortunately, however, the market cross has been turned into a mini traffic circus, with plastic bollards and white arrows on blue circles.

Trying to upstage the ancient cross further are signposts of different shapes and signs pointing to various destinations. Before approaching the centre of the burgh competent drivers must surely consult their maps. If removing these signs would cause drivers to lose their way, the townspeople of Melrose need not feel guilty, for drivers who did would deserve to get lost.

Architecture and conservation

Traditional town centres have nourished local character over the years by virtue of their own abiding life force. Buildings which are the major repositories of local character are the result of the endeavours of past generations, and consequently the town centres have become steeped in humanity. If this character is to be sustained in the future, many of the older buildings will have to be retained and, from time to time, buildings will have to be replaced(**87**). A policy of conservation and renewal will

safeguard the local character beloved by citizens, but it demands skill in the technical work of conserving the old buildings and architectural tact in introducing the buildings of the future.

Conservation in this context does not involve only buildings of high architectural merit. Some buildings in shopping and commercial centres, especially some recent examples, are so cheap and makeshift in design and materials that nothing short of their removal should be contemplated for their future. These apart, simple Scottish buildings in stone and lime – even though they might not be adopted into the Secretary of State's listed building categories – contribute along with more stylish examples to that suffusion of architecture which gives character to Scottish High Streets. If the merits of a centre are assessed only on the basis of examples of outstanding architecture, or of famous architects who might have designed them, the character of the whole town centre can pass unrecognised.

Character can only be fully appreciated when a High Street, its plan and all its buildings are comprehended as an entity. The presence of buildings belonging to so many ages, from the eighteenth century onwards, positively reinforces character. Not all architects agree on this, however. For instance, the respected authors of *Building Scotland* unfavourably compare the multi-styled architecture of Princes Street with the Rue de Rivoli in Paris: 'Princes Street bickers from end to end, an unseemly brawl', whereas 'the Rue de Rivoli quietly draws the passer-by to the shops that lie within its graceful arcade'. The regimented regularity of the Rue de Rivoli has the character of a street imposed on a town by an overbearing authority – a type of town planning which the ethos of Scotland emphatically rejects.

163

Princes Street has suffered from two major planning errors. First, there was the failure to prevent the destruction of some of the best of the impressive nineteenth-century buildings, for example: the former home of the New Club; the Life Association building (containing the Methven Simpson premises) which was designed by Sir Charles Barry (1855) and inspired by a Venetian palazzo; and the old Boots building, with its rich façade of statuary. Second, building since the war has demonstrated how difficult it is to match that elegance and superiority of the earlier façades which the eminence of Princes Street demands(**47**, p.97, **73**, p.134). Dull repetition or blatant commercial license are not the solutions to the mistakes which have been made in Princes Street.

Conservation has to be based on correct techniques. These have been greatly advanced in recent years but are not always employed. Chimney heads are removed on gables facing the streets or are rebuilt in brick and roughcast with the rest of the gable in stone. Red English chimney cans are used to replace the traditional golden fireclay. The misguided procedure of roughcasting old rubble stonework still persists even when it is coated with the soot of years gone past. Old stone buildings so treated are applauded in their modern white covering by critics who remain silent when the soot begins to permeate through to the surface, leaving a spectacle of tawdry decrepitude in place of the fine craftsmanship which was so unwisely blotted out(**87**).

Deterioration behind the front streets too often continues when choked and leaking rainwater pipes and gutters spill water down the walls, which become stained and saturated externally and subject to dry rot internally. Stone cleaning is permissible but only if the composition and texture of the stone will permit it without recourse to grinding.

The problems of conserving old buildings submit to solutions more readily than those pertaining to new buildings. The general requirements, the restrictions on lengths and heights, the use of suitable material, adherence to building lines, and the quality of appearing 'at home' in the street are generally understood. To avoid disharmony with its neighbours a new building should not need to ape the attributes of older styles, such as crow-stepped gables, sash-and-case windows, Georgian astragals and other such details, although some experts do not accept this approach(**88**). The temptation which confronts many architects is their desire to offer a shining new personal statement in architectural terms without thought as to whether a town's High Street happens to be the most suitable platform for the performance. Such architects feel that if they have to suppress personal expression in their design in order to make a building 'at home' in the street, they will have failed. It needs a genius to make a building that speaks emphatically in the

88 Selkirk: Kirk Wynd. An example of rebuilding on the fringe of the market-place on the sites of former old but non-listed buildings, while retaining the original historic streets.

architectural language of the future intelligible when it is set down among buildings that speak in the architectural language of the past. What may be needed is for architects venturing into Scottish High Streets to exercise a degree of restraint, and study the practice of urbanculture, so that twentieth-century buildings can exist harmoniously with the buildings of the past without being too assertive. In general terms more cannot be said. Just as towns have their own individual character, new buildings need individual rules.

Towns also have individual colour. New buildings in High Streets where granite or sandstone predominates should be fronted in these materials. For the preservation of character it is usually highly desirable that the stone should be of a colour in harmony with what has been employed in the past. For example, red stone appears frequently in towns such as Dumfries, Dunbar, East Linton(**89**), Ayr, Arbroath, Lochmaben, Johnstone, Dumbarton and many more. Pink and pinkish-grey stone walls are found in Brechin, Perth, Forfar, Callander(**90**), Stonehaven and others. Cream stone of various hues from dark honey to light cream predominates over much of the country. Neutral grey stone is uncommon, contrary to popular belief, but examples may be seen in some whinstone areas such as Lauder and Auchtermuchty. Painted walls typify some of the west coast towns, the Fife coastal burghs and small towns like

89 East Linton. The main street winds downhill in the traditional Scottish style and terminates in pantiled roofs. Together with the landscape of the rising ground on the horizon, it makes a perfect urban scene.

Cromarty(**91**), Eddleston, and at Peebles, where some black and white painting has been adopted(**69**, p.131). Outstanding character derives from granite walls in Aberdeenshire and Banffshire towns, flagstone in Orkney and Caithness and whinstone in some Border towns.

Some towns would benefit greatly if windows and doors were painted in appropriate colours. To be correct colours need to be in harmony with the background of stone. In centres where wall painting is traditional the selection of colours should be made by matching stonework, paving, slates and so on onsite with colour cards on a bright, sunless day. Colouring in the town centres should be regarded with the same care that an artist takes at his easel. In most towns the basic wall colours are the pale sandy yellow in some areas tending to parchment, in others to honey colour. There, the paintwork should be white, cream and tints ranging from pale yellow through to rich orpiment, especially with dark Scotch slates. In towns where reds and pink stone is prominent, the colours may be light pinkish grey, pastel reds, black at details and silver greys. It would be helpful to owners if suitable colour cards were prepared by the planning authorities for the various towns in their areas where wall painting is established. Door and window colours are better selected individually for each separate building.

For a long time after 1945 white buildings became the passion of modern Scottish architects and later some Planning Officers. Despite the fact that white buildings very seldom ever played any

90 Callander. A holiday town where it has been appreciated that all the buildings must look at home in the scenic splendour of the surroundings.

role in Scottish burgh tradition, some mature professionals still seem to find difficulty in giving up their infatuation. The vogue grew first on the Continent, where the brightness gives white building a dazzling effect. The professional black and white architectural photographers began developing techniques which filtered pale blue Scottish skies to an almost black intensity and left light-coloured building portrayed in the dazzling glare of the Mediterranean(**92**) – as if by magic the climate of Crete had been brought to Britain, and architects filled their brochures with attractive photographs of their productions to prove it. In their minds the photographic image took precedence over reality.

This post-war vogue is mentioned because a new craze for eager young architects to seize upon is beginning to manifest itself. The bright harsh colouring of television and video has its admirers and has begun to show its influence on property and buildings in England. Traditional colouring in Scotland's towns has derived from the natural colours of the local materials, which happen to blend with the soil, soft light, delicate colouring

91 Cromarty. A delightful small, eighteenth-century town miraculously preserved and sturdily built to withstand the sea gales and the attentions of future would-be demolishers or improvers.

of clouds and the Scotch mist of the country. If this inherited characteristic of the burghs is to be conserved, the authorities should begin to prepare themselves to resist the theatrical extremities of the raw reds, the violence of purple, the acid greens, the gaudy orange and the electric blues.

Large-scale commercial premises

A unity of character in the historic towns has persisted because each building and re-building of the frontage always adhered to the original widths of the plots laid down at about the twelfth century. In some instances in the eighteenth-century some longer frontages were devised by combining several plot widths to provide longer fronts, but these still were built adopting local stone and the architectural style of the neighbouring building. In the twentieth century longer frontages are again in demand. In relation to character this raises problems which become greatly intensified if higher densities are also called for – such as in offices and departmental stores, and even housing. When the promoters of such projects are permitted to build in an old established street, the results are calamitous for character. The post-war building at Inverness has dwarfed the few adjacent older houses, shops and trees into pathetic insignificance(**86**, p.160). In a few years the familiar unity of the older street which comfortingly reached right back to the foundation of the town has disappeared. The new constructions have no point of contact with the past. They have moved in as if from another planet – an ever-present warning of the awesome power of those who can conjure them so effortlessly out of an urge to make money. Similarly, the graceless intrusion of the fifteen-storey builders' houses rearing above the two-storey and three-storey buildings in the main square of the planned town of Johnstone illustrates what ignorance of sound practice in urbanculture can produce. Had the tall building been composed with the skill and artistry of the cathedral builders, Johnstone would have been richly blessed, but the medieval builders built their towers to the glory of God, a sublime conception which for national house builders presumably surpasses all understanding. If there is validity in the saying that modern society gets the buildings and towns it deserves, it must be hoped that more critical responses towards town centres will be forthcoming. Already, adverse reactions to unnecessary tall building in Scotland are having effect. Tall office blocks at town centres other than in the cities should be banned. Three or four storeys for offices are practicable and economical, and that has to be the rule. If the lengths exceed the usual traditional urban unit of about 23 feet (7 metres), blocks should be divided and the parts differentiated to maintain the established rhythm of the High Street frontage.

In the eighteenth-century plans the unit frontages averaged about thirty feet (9.10 metres), permitting larger and usually taller replacements. Modern larger frontages with almost interminable bands of glass alternating with equal bands of uninterrupted walling are inadvisable even where the productions are the standard 'house styles' of the notable architects concerned.

92 Edinburgh: No. 64 Princes Street, post-war building. A building which does not seem to try to approach the stylish elegance which Princes Street demands.

The trend of national retail companies for building large shops in towns poses difficulties where scale of building contributes to character. The solution being adopted in many such towns is to position the large supermarket or shopping centre beyond the traditional shopping area. This policy leads to the closing of local shops and the property agents' 'For Sale' boards which have in recent years become an alarming sight in High Streets. Frank supermarket operators acknowledge that in such circumstances loss of local shops is inevitable. It has been claimed, however, that when a large supermarket is set in the main shopping street, small shops adjacent selling home-baked produce, fresh unpackaged food, fish and meat, and providing services such as shoe repairing, dry cleaning, and so on benefit from the custom of the supermarket shoppers. Keeping the supermarkets within the centres may be the better policy, but it needs to conform to the character of each town, and the areas behind the High Street will need to be opened up for car parking. All this is possible.

Modern chain stores sometimes adopt a policy of standard fascias, lettering and architectural style – as if every town in Britain should aim at national uniformity and become indistinguishable from other towns. Such a policy signals the ultimate demise of local individualism. Standard fascias and architecture are inimicable to character. Facing-brick frontages, all glass walls and red English plain roof tiles do not look at home in any shopping street in Scotland – even in Princes Street where, as has been pointed out, good manners and elegant style have been lacking in recent changes(**92, 93**).

General amenity and the role of planners

General amenity in towns consists of the art of creating more pleasant surroundings for buildings. This is achieved by ridding towns of unnecessary clutter while ensuring that large spaces are not left empty and their surfaces left unrelieved by a monotonous, grey Macadamised expanse. If the spaces are furnished with a few monuments or pieces of sculpture and decorated with shrubs and flowers, large market-places look very welcoming. Kelso has its handsome square laid in stone sets(**78**, p.147); Irvine put down a well planned layout of coloured paving; Arbroath, the home of the beautiful stone flags, has paved its shopping area in concrete flags(**84**, p.159); Stromness retains its Orkney flagstone; while the National Trust for Scotland arranged the much loved cobbles for Culross. Dalkeith paved its shopping square at Jarnac Court and Eskdaill Court is furnished with trees, flowers, sculptures and a low, open rotunda with seats. Dalkeith's centre demonstrates how within twenty-five years young trees protected in the shelter of three-storey buildings grow straight and tall and well shaped as they reach up

93 Edinburgh: No. 101 Princes Street, post-war building. A design-conscious building which would be more at home somewhere else in Britain.

to the sun and sky.

Surviving market crosses return to their rightful prominence when parked cars and road signs are removed, but these monuments should not be flippantly treated like the cross at Dingwall(**39**, p.83), where the base of the cross has been buried in a heap of concrete in which large stones are bedded – looking like a stirring stick stuck in a heap of cold, stiff porridge. Urban history benefits from the use of paving to mark the site of former crosses or trons if money cannot be found to pay for their replacement. The marked out plan of the tron in sets at the foot of Castle Hill in the Royal Mile was recently removed when the unworkable mini-roundabout was formed. Presumably the authorities did not know what they were destroying.

Edinburgh for a considerable period prohibited the hanging of shop signs from impairing the fronts of shops and buildings in main streets. The wisdom of this policy had a lasting effect. The West of Scotland has fared less well. Newton Stewart, a well established attractive town and a tourist centre, displays a large collection in the space of a few buildings in the main street. It is doubtful if one more cup of coffee, glass of beer or Coke is drunk, or more newspapers read, or more mortgages obtained as a result. It is certain that the attraction of the town, an important factor in its success, is diminished and cheapened. Many other centres have been afflicted with this fashion, probably because when one bank, building society, shop or bar acquires a sign others feel obliged to follow.

Some of the smaller towns have submitted to the affront of wooden poles with telephone or power wires strung along the roadside through the main street. The delightful town of Cromarty has them rising well above the eaves of the houses. Whithorn, a medieval planned town associated with one of the earliest Christian settlements, has been shamefully desecrated by wooden poles and wires on both sides of the street – as many as sixteen within a short length of view. It is an irony that had the timber been growing as trees, the man with the saw would have given them his attention long before now.

Fortunately, town centres in Scotland in general are not afflicted with walls disfigured by posters and spray painting. Yet even in this matter improvements are needed. Edinburgh's Royal Mile suffers during the Festival when windows, walls and lamp-posts are used for advertising posters and stickers. Young theatrical and artistic companies treat Scotland's historic street with disrespect, and return to England leaving the mess for others to clear. Equally unfortunate is the invasion of travel agents into town and city streets, where the insides of shop windows are plastered with advertising posters. If persuasion cannot induce these agents to remove such eyesores, legislation may have to be adopted to give planning authorities power to have them compulsorily removed. The legislation would also be profitably applied to the window advertisements in some supermarkets. This situation, like many other blemishes in town centres is trivial and cheaply remedied, but left to persist because of apathy.

Modern legislation controlling change and growth in towns developed from early Town Planning Acts up to the Town and Country Planning (Scotland) Act 1932. From that time several limited but valid schemes were prepared and others were in process when 1939 stopped all planning. For several years after 1945, Scots were promised visions of revitalised towns and exciting new life, despite rationing and thousands without houses. In 1945 and 1947 new Planning Acts laid the cold, dead hand of bureaucracy on the new ideas being born, and they perished. Planning legislation excelled in creating a system of controls in a proliferation of Orders, Statutory Instruments, Circulars and Acts (including that of 1968) which were more preventive than creative. In legislation it is easier to say 'Thou shalt not' than to say 'Thou shalt act'.

The post-war Acts directly led to Town Planning Officers frustrating reasonable proposals for new building or for extensions by owners wishing to revive their business or improve their houses – activities urgently needed in order to refresh towns after the war. The situation alarmed Sir Frank Mears, whose technique of planning towns was founded on resolving apparent conflicts in a town plan in order to assimilate them. He did not favour outright refusal. If resolving conflicts was not feasible, he sought for alternative sites. In 1949 he adumbrated a

Moratorium in Planning to ease the frustration that planning in its new powerful status was causing. He did not question the need for the intelligent and orderly direction of urban development, but there could be too much planning, and too many planners were threatening to tie up the future in a network of fixed ideas. These Planning Officers, some understandably inexperienced and impractical, did not make sufficient allowance for economical and social changes which can render the finest plans out of date. Mears saw planning as a provisional business, and continuous adaptation of long-term plans was necessary. Planning, he pointed out, is subject to unpredictable mutations.

These warnings were voiced nearly forty years ago and planning departments are still referring to the Development Plans and refusing proposals because they do not fit their scheme. Planners have not the gift of prophecy and cannot see round the next corner. When they arrive at such a point they should be allowed to adjust their plan if an unforeseeable situation comes before them which they could not have anticipated at the time their schemes were produced.

Planning appeals still grind their way through the costly processes, often to be rejected because the proposal conflicted with the approved town plan. A planning appeal is a most unsatisfactory mode of reaching a decision. It focusses on every point that can be mustered for and against a proposal in ridiculous detail, and exaggerates the points under consideration to the detriment of obtaining a balanced view of the whole town or district. A planning appeal represents not a case of failing to see the wood for the trees, but of failing to see even the tree for the leaf.

Planning appeals should only arise when applicants will not agree to a justifiable adjustment, or when planning departments are satisfied that proposals would seriously reduce standards in a town. Negotiations would lead more quickly to an adjusted solution if lay observers, say the Chief Executive and the applicant's legal agent, were present to assess the merits and defects of argument and counter-argument. When acting for planning authorities himself, Sir Frank Mears thought discussions with applicants were essential before any proposals were submitted, and it is significant that he rarely advised outright refusal. The town planning scheme he prepared was approved without any objection or public inquiry because he personally met all the representatives of the various organisations in the town to enable him to produce an acceptable solution. The authority as a consequence had the support of most of the community, an important factor because planning towns is in the end most of all about people.

More disturbing than the difficulties about legislation and

procedure is the neglect of imaginative thinking in the preparation of town plans. Planning education courses perhaps over-react to the danger of unrealistic ideas about changing towns for the better. Emphasis is laid on the Geddes dictum of 'survey before plan'. Too literal an interpretation of this approach tends to convince some planners that the plans of the future should not reflect any ideas that have not emerged from the survey data they have accumulated so meticulously. They dismiss such ideas as 'aspirational'. In the story of Scotland's towns from the twelfth century onwards men have been inspired to plan new towns, to renew and enlarge them with creative force, to use their imaginations to beautify and enhance them. Today people in villages, towns and cities are awakening to the opportunities for conserving them, making them more attractive and trying to protect them from inappropriate alteration or additions. Scotland may be on the threshold of a great new age of towns. When the people are preparing for it, professional planners should be ready, equipped to lead.

Further Reading and Bibliography

Titles marked with an asterisk are recommended for further reading. Also recommended are the local histories of burghs which have been published since the nineteenth century. There are too many to be included in a general list, but most local libraries have copies. Many modern guides (such as those in the R.I.A.S./Landmark series) are excellent, but they concentrate on individual examples of architecture rather than on a comprehensive view of towns and streets, and to that extent they are less relevant to the subject under review.

*Adams, I. H., *The Making of Urban Scotland* (London 1978).

*Alcock, L., Talbot, E., Turner Simpson, A., Gourlay, R., and Stevenson, S., *The Scottish Burgh Survey:* 53 reports (Glasgow, 1976–84).

Anderson, A. R., *Augustinian and Benedictine Monasteries in Scotland* (Glasgow, 1954).

Ashworth, J. H., *et al* (ed.), *Edinburgh's Place in Scientific Progress* (Edinburgh and London, 1921).

Barrie, D. A., *The City of Dundee Illustrated* (Dundee, 1890).

*Bell, G., *Blackfriars' Wynd Analyzed* (Edinburgh, 1850).

*Bell, G., *Day and Night in the Wynds of Edinburgh* (Edinburgh, 1850).

*Black, W. G., *The Scots Mercat Cross* (Glasgow and Edinburgh, 1928).

Bowie, J. A., *The Future of Scotland* (London and Edinburgh, 1939).

Brotchie, A. W., and Herd, J. J., *Getting Around Old Dundee* (Dundee, 1984).

*Brown, J. (ed.)., *Scottish Society in the Fifteenth Century* (London, 1977).

*Brown, P. H. (ed.), *Early Travellers in Scotland* (Edinburgh, 1891).

*Butchart, R., *Prints and Drawings of Edinburgh* (Edinburgh, 1955).

The Marquis of Bute, *A Plea for Scotland's Architectural Heritage* (Edinburgh, 1936).

Butt, J., *Industrial Archaeology of Scotland* (Newton Abbot, 1967).

Butt, J., and Gordon G., *Strathclyde: Changing Horizons* (Edinburgh, 1985).

Cadell of Grange, H. M., *Industrial Possibilities of the Forth Estuary* (Edinburgh, 1918).

*Campbell, R. H., and Skinner, A. J. (ed.), *The Origin and Nature of the Scottish Enlightenment* (Edinburgh, 1982).

Cant, J., *The Muses' Threnodie* (Perth, 1774).

*Cant, R. G., *et al.*, *Old St Andrews* (St Andrews, 1943).

*Cant, R. G., and Lindsay, I. G., *Old Elgin* (Elgin, 1946).

*Cant, R. G., and Lindsay, I. G., *Old Stirling* (Edinburgh and London, 1948).

*Cant, R. G., *Old Moray* (Elgin, 1948).

Carr, H., *The Masons and the Burgh* (London, 1954).

*Chambers, R., *The Traditions of Edinburgh* (Edinburgh, 1868).

Clyde, J. L., Whitson, Sir Thomas, and Pollock, Sir Donald, *Report of the Advisory Committee on City Development, Edinburgh* (Edinburgh, 1943).

Colvin, H., 'The Beginnings of the Architectural Profession in Scotland', *Architectural History*, vol. 29 (1986).

*Corporation of the City of Glasgow, *Municipal Glasgow and its Evolution and Enterprises* (Glasgow, 1910).

Cox, E., *History of Gardening in Scotland* (London, 1930).

Daiches D., *Glasgow* (London, 1977).

Deighton, J. S., *Eaglesham: an Earl's Creation* (London, 1974).

Dickinson, W. Croft, *Scotland from the Earliest Times to 1603* (Edinburgh and London, 1960).

*Donaldson, G., *Scotland: James V–James VII* (Edinburgh, 1965).

*Drummond, J., *Old Edinburgh* (Edinburgh and London, 1879).

*Duncan, A. A. M., *Scotland: the Making of the Kingdom* (Edinburgh, 1975).

*Fawcett, R., *Scottish Medieval Churches* (Edinburgh, 1985).

*Geddes, P., *Edinburgh and its Region: Geographical and Historical* (Edinburgh, 1902).

*Geddes, P., *A Study in City Development* (Edinburgh and London, 1904).

*Geddes, P., *The Survey of Cities* (London, 1908).

*Geddes, P., *City Deterioration and the Need for a City Survey* (Philadelphia, 1909).

*Geddes, P., *Civic Survey of Edinburgh* (Edinburgh, 1911).

*Geddes, P., *Cities in Evolution* (London, 1915).

*Geddes, P., *Cities and Town Planning Exhibition* (Edinburgh, 1911).

*Geddes, P., and Mears, F. C., *Town Planning Towards City Development: A Report to the Director of Indore* (Indore, 1918).

*Geddes, P., *et al.*, 'Beginnings of a Survey of Edinburgh', *Scottish Geographical Magazine*, vol. 35 (1919).

Gibb, A., *Glasgow, The Making of a City* (London, 1978).

*Gifford, J., McWilliam, C., and Walker, D., *The Buildings of Scotland: Edinburgh* (Harmondsworth, 1984).

Gordon, G. (ed.), *Perspectives of the Scottish City* (1985).

*Gordon, G., and Dicks, B., *Scottish Urban History* (Aberdeen, 1983).

*Grant Education Co., *A Scots History of Britain* (London and Glasgow, 1930).

Gunn, J., and Newbigin, M. I. (ed.), *The City of Glasgow: its Origin, Growth and Development* (Edinburgh, 1921).

Hamilton, T. W., *How Greenock Grew* (Greenock, 1947).

Hammond, M., *Castles of Britain. Volume 2: Scotland* (London, 1964).

Hannah, J. C., *The Story of Scotland in Stone* (Edinburgh, 1964).

Holdsworth, R. (ed.), *Excavations in the Medieval Burgh of Perth* (Edinburgh, 1988).

*Home, B. J., *Old Houses in Edinburgh* (Edinburgh, 1985).

*Howard, E., *Garden Cities of Tomorrow* (Eastbourne, 1902).

*Innes, C. (ed.), *Ancient Laws and Customs of the Burghs of Scotland, AD 1124–1424* (Edinburgh, 1868).

*Irons, J. C., *Leith and its Antiquities*, vols. 1 and 2 (Edinburgh, 1897).

James, R. F., *Lauder: its Kirk and its People* (Galashiels, 1973).

Laing, L., *The Archaeology of Late Celtic Britain and Ireland, circa 400 to 1200 AD* (London, 1975).

*Lamb, A. C., *Dundee* (Dundee, 1895).

Lannon, T., *The Making of Modern Stirling* (Stirling, 1983).

*Lindsay, I. G., *Burgh Architecture* (Edinburgh, 1948).

*Lindsay, I. G., *Architecture in Scotland* (London, 1948).

*Lindsay, I. G., *Old Edinburgh* (Edinburgh and London, 1939).

Lindsay, M., *Portrait of Glasgow* (London, 1972).

*Littlejohn, H. O., *Report on the Sanitary Condition of Edinburgh* (Edinburgh, 1865).

Local Government Board for Scotland, *Provisions of Houses for the Working Classes after the War* (Edinburgh and Aberdeen, 1918).

Lynch, M. (ed.), *The Early Modern Town in Scotland* (London, 1987).

*Mackay, W., *Life in Inverness in the Sixteenth Century* (Aberdeen, 1911).

Mackinnon, J., *The Social and Industrial History of Scotland* (London and Glasgow, 1920).

McLaren, T., *Early Plans of Perth* (Perth, 1943).

*McNeill, P., *Tranent and its Surroundings* (Edinburgh and Glasgow, 1884).

McNeill, P., and Nicholson, R. (ed.), *An Historical Atlas of Scotland, circa 400– 1600* (St Andrews, 1975).

MacRae, E. J., *City of Edinburgh: the Royal Mile* (Edinburgh, 1946).

*McWilliam, C., *Scottish Townscape* (Glasgow, 1975).

*Mears, F. C., *Measured Drawings of Lawnmarket and Castle Hill by Thomas Hamilton* (Edinburgh, 1923).

*Mears, F. C., *The City of Edinburgh* (Edinburgh, 1931).

Mears, F. C., 'An Experiment in Planning for Agriculture and Industry', *Journal of the Royal Society of Arts,* vol. 89 (1941).

Mears, F. C., 'Notes on a Medieval Burgess's House, Inverkeithing', *Proceedings of the Society of Antiquaries of Scotland,* vol. 47 (191213).

Mears, F. C., and Russell, J., *The New Town of Edinburgh* (Edinburgh, 1939).

*Mumford, L., *The Culture of Cities and the City in History* (London, 1938; rpt. 1961).

Nichol, J. and D., *Cities and Towns of Scotland Illustrated* (Montrose, 1843).

*Nicholson, R., *Scotland: The Later Middle Ages* (Edinburgh, 1974).

Ochme, R., and Hibbert, A., *Old European Cities* (London, n.d.).

Paterson, J., *History of the Regality of Musselburgh* (Musselburgh, 1857).

Phillipson, N. T., and Mitchison, R., *Scotland in the Age of Improvement* (Edinburgh and London, 1970).

Piggot, S. (ed.), *The Prehistoric Peoples of Scotland* (London, 1962).

*Pryde, G. S., *The Burghs of Scotland: A Critical List* (London, 1965).

Rasmussen, S. E., *Towns and Buildings* (Liverpool, 1957).

*Reiach, A., and Hurd, R., *Building Scotland* (Edinburgh, 1944).

Ritchie, R. L. G., *The Normans in Scotland* (Edinburgh 1954).

Rogers, C., *Social Life in Scotland from Early to Recent Times* (London, 1884).

Romanes, R., *Lauder* (Lauder, 1903).

Scott-Moncrieff, G. (ed.), *The Stones of Scotland* (London, 1938).

Scott-Moncrieff, G., *The Buildings of Scotland* (Edinburgh, 1944).

Shaw, G., *Water Power in Scotland, 1550–1870* (Edinburgh, 1984).

Shearer, R. S., *Stirling, Historical and Descriptive* (Stirling, 1897).

*Shirley, G. W., *The Growth of a Scottish Burgh: A Study in the Early History of Dumfries* (Dumfries, 1915).

*Sinclair, Sir John (ed.), *Statistical Account of Scotland,* 21 vols. (Edinburgh, 1791–99).

*Sinclair, Sir John (ed.), *The New Statistical Account of Scotland,* 15 vols. (Edinburgh and London, 1845).

Sinclair, Sir John (ed.), *The Third Statistical Account of Scotland* (Edinburgh, 1953).

*Small, J. W., *Scottish Market Crosses* (Edinburgh, 1900).

Smeaton, A., *Reports on Acts and Procedures of the Town Council of Edinburgh* (Edinburgh, 1769).

*Smith, G. G., *The Days of James IV, 1488–1513* (London, 1900).

*Smout, T. C., *A History of the Scottish People, 1560–1830* (Glasgow, 1973).

Special Committee Company of Merchants, *The Development of Edinburgh,* (Edinburgh, 1919).

Stones, J. A. (ed.), *A Tale of Two Burghs* (Aberdeen, 1987).

Storer, J. and H. S., *Views on Edinburgh and its Vicinity,* 2 vols (London, 1820).

Strawhern, J., *The History of Irvine: Royal Burgh and New Town* (Edinburgh, 1985).

Sutcliffe, A. (ed.), *Multi-Storey Living* (London, 1974).

Taylor, G., *Urban Geography* (London, 1949).

Traquair, R., and Mears, F. C., *Public Monuments: The Blue Blanket* (Edinburgh, 1912).

University of Edinburgh, *Proposals for Future Development of the University of Edinburgh* (Edinburgh, 1947).

Unwin, R., *Nothing Gained by Overcrowding* (London, 1918).

Whittington, G., and Whyte, I. D., *An Historical Geography of Scotland* (London, 1983).

Wilkie, J., *Historic Musselburgh* (Edinburgh, 1919).

*Wood, J., *Atlas: Plans of Scottish Towns* (Edinburgh, 1828).

*Wood, J., *Descriptive Account of the Principal Towns in Scotland* (Edinburgh, 1828).

Wood, S., and Patrick, J., *History of the Grampian Landscape* (Aberdeen, 1982).

Worsdall, F., *The Tenement* (Edinburgh, 1979).

Worsdall, F., *The City that Disappeared* (Glasgow, 1981).

Wyness, F., *Aberdeen: Century of Change* (Aberdeen, 1971).

*Youngson, A. J., *The Making of Classical Edinburgh* (Edinburgh, 1966).

Index to Towns